BDSM Relationships

How They Work

BDSM Relationships

How They Work

Peter Masters

Books in the present series:

Understanding BDSM Relationships

BDSM Relationships - How They Work

BDSM Relationships - Pitfalls and Obstacles

Also by Peter Masters:

The Control Book

*Look Into My Eyes - How To Use Hypnosis To
Bring Out The Best In Your Sex Life*

*This Curious Human Phenomenon - An
exploration of some uncommonly explored aspects
of BDSM*

Cover art by Peter Masters

http://www.peter-masters.com/

ISBN 978-1-4774-6766-4

Contents

Chapter 1

Introduction

In book one of this series, *Understanding BDSM Relationships*, I looked at BDSM wants and needs, and at how they get satisfied in the context of a BDSM relationship. It's important to note that when I talk about a relationship this can include any sort of connection between two BDSM-practising folk, whether they live together in a full-on, 24/7, master/slave household, whether they are a full-time couple who only occasionally dally in BDSM, or whether they are two friends who mainly meet up at BDSM parties and who only play together there.

One reason why I'm interested in relationships is that there's a lot of literature available about BDSM as it affects or is practised by a single person, but not so much on the role of a long-, or even short-term relationship and how it can influence the pleasure and satisfaction BDSM can provide. I think that this is a great shortcoming because when you look around at what other BDSM folk are doing, there are an awful lot of them either in, or looking for, long-term relationships, even if this is just establishing a circle of trusted friends with whom to explore. If a BDSM scene were able to be satisfying and rewarding on its own then you'd expect that there'd be a lot more one-night stands than there are. Instead, it looks remarkably as if being in some sort of relationship with someone can significantly add to or improve what we get out of BDSM, perhaps to the point where such a relationship is a necessity for many people.

In this book, I want to move from understanding to the actual doing. I want to look at how what we do, how we behave, and how we communicate affect our ability to establish and to maintain a full and satisfying BDSM-based relationship with someone. To some extent this will include what can go wrong, but I will be addressing that particular topic in more detail in book three of this series, *BDSM Relationships - Pitfalls and Obstacles*. In the what-can-go-right department in this book, I'm particularly interested to explore how what we do influences and modulates the penetration and engagement we experience with our partners. Penetration and engagement, you may recall, are two of the three pillars of BDSM relationships which I introduced in book one.

Broadly speaking then, this book is about stepping on from understanding BDSM and BDSM relationships. It's about making concrete:

- Our motivations—our wants and needs, and

- How what we do meets or satisfies those wants and needs within the context of a relationship.

To this end, I'll be going through a wide range of motivations, wants, and needs in detail, and I'll be looking at how a comprehensive list of common and not-so-common **BDSM** activities each work to satisfy or meet those needs.

Chapter 2

Trust, honesty, openness, communication, and all that stuff

The success of any BDSM relationship is going to depend on communication. It never will be enough to be good at flogging or to be able to have endless orgasms if what you're trying to do is have a successful and satisfying relationship with someone.

Communication is what establishes a connection with your partner. It isn't just words, but is also actions and gestures. If you're a dominant or top then communicating can include how you strike with a flogger, how you tie knots, how you cut your partner with a blade, how you drip wax on them, and so on. Each action that your partner experiences from you sends them a message and tells them something.

If you're a submissive or bottom, then how you breath while being flogged, how you wince as you are cut, or how you kneel while serving your partner a drink, also send your partner a message.

After compatibility, communication is about the most important component of a relationship which works well, which flows smoothly, which has little or no conflict, and which is deeply satisfying and rewarding for the people involved.

2.1   Openness and honesty

Openness and honesty are critical to getting BDSM to work. This might sound really, really obvious—and it's something I mention often—but it's not always easy to be open and honest, either with yourself or with your partner. Many things can get in the way.

Openness and honesty are very frequently more important in BDSM relationships than they are in vanilla relationships. As I've mentioned before, vanilla relationships are about doing things with your partner. They share with you in external things which are stimulating, interesting, or rewarding. This includes going to the movies, going out to dinner, going for walks, going shopping, and even raising kids together. Little of the "goodness" in these things comes from your partner. At the movies, it's the film you watch. At dinner, it's the food you eat. While out walking, it's the weather and the scenery. And with kids, it's, well..., the kids.

In vanilla relationships you aren't so dependent on your partner to have rewarding or powerful experiences. As long as you both go to the right places or events—and as long as you don't get in each other's way—a great time will be had by one and all.

On the other hand, in BDSM relationships you are completely dependent on your partner for your scenes and activities to work. If you aren't focussed, or your partner isn't focussed, then the experiences can quickly become hollow and unsatisfying. And what you need to be focussed on is each other.

Importantly, your partner is presumably trying to push your buttons so that you get the most out of whatever-it-is that you're doing together. For them to push the right buttons they need you to be completely open and honest with them.

This is where the problems can start.

If your partner is particularly desirable and there's some doubt about how long they'll stay interested, you might be tempted to present yourself in a way that might be more attractive to them. For example, if they are a keen bondage aficionado then you might be inclined to exaggerate your interest in bondage when actually you prefer flogging. While in vanilla-land this might be an effective strategy to keep this new partner around long enough for them to find out that you're actually the greatest thing since sliced bread, in BDSM-land this is fairly devastating. Your new BDSM partner will be trying to push the buttons you've indicated you have even though you actually have other buttons. You end up faking responses, and this is not a good long-term strategy for a relationship.

Another thing which can get in the way of openness and honesty is ego. Admitting to weakness, or lack of skill, or lack of knowledge in a particular area can sometimes be hard. This can also be dangerous if your ego tries to get you to exaggerate how much experience you have in some of the more challenging areas of BDSM such as heavy impact play, cutting, piercing, mummification, or breath play.

2.2   Communication during play

Communication is important to let your partner know what's working and what isn't. Importantly, it's also one of the key parts of engaging your partner.

If you immerse yourself in your BDSM activities—such as soaking up the thuds when your partner is flogging your back, or focussing intently on the patterns you're creating when you cane your partner's rear end—then your partner may not be getting something they need. They may be hungering for a feeling of being connected to you. If they're not facing you and you're not making any sounds yourself, they'll probably not feel connected at all.

While forcing yourself to moan, "Oh! Baby!!!", all the time might be excessive, making noises and murmuring comments as things progress can be of immense help in telling your partner: a) that you're still there, and b) how you're feeling.

Moans are often good value in this regard, but don't limit yourself just to sounds. Wriggle, writhe, move your feet, and change position to improve the angle of attack. Say things quietly to yourself, but loudly enough for them to hear, such as, "Mmmm. That's nice.", "I love the way you turn red!", or "That's making me so hot!"

Making sounds or communicating may not feel 100% natural for you. You may even be concerned that your noises and wriggles may be a distraction for your partner. Talk to them and find out how they feel.

2.3   Negotiation

Some days BDSM is just not going to come easy.

You might not be in the mood, you may be tired, or some particular activity your partner is looking for really squicks you out. When this is the case, don't just shake your head and say no because this can make your partner feel rejected. Instead sit and talk with them. Look for a solution to this problem.

If you're tired, maybe something light will work for you. Alternatively, plan a session for the next day so your partner is sure you're still interested in them and so they have something to look forward to.

If the particular activity your partner has in mind really puts you off, there may be an alternative which will work for them just as well and which you'll also find satisfying and rewarding.

The important thing is to talk. Be open about how you feel. Be open to the suggestions or ideas from your partner.

Chapter 3

Meeting people

Before you can have a BDSM relationship, you need to meet people with whom such a relationship is possible. Finding a BDSM partner can be very challenging for a number of reasons. Firstly, very few people stroll around wearing head-to-toe latex or full BDSM leathers, nor are BDSM weekend or nocturnal escapades common topics of conversation around the average water cooler. BDSM is instead more underground and this makes it challenging to find someone with similar interests to your own.

Secondly, newcomers to BDSM—those people just discovering BDSM urges in themselves, or those who have only now decided to act on them—frequently have no idea that there are others like them "out there". They don't know about any opportunities to meet others, to get experience, to attend workshops, to get skills training, and to share ideas and thoughts with other people who have the same drives and desires.

Indeed, it's not uncommon for people to have their first BDSM experiences totally ignorant of the fact that there are many hundreds of thousands of people actively pursuing the very same things they are only just getting to know.

Because BDSM is often associated with sex, places you can look for information about BDSM activities in your geographical area include articles and advertisements in your local sex-positive newspapers, checking noticeboards, or by asking in any local shops which sell sex aids.

BDSM can also have an affiliation with the gay, lesbian, and bisexual (GLB) community, and even if you're not gay, lesbian, or bisexual, it might be worth contacting any GLB groups in your area, or checking out their newsletters or newspapers to see if they have any outreach programs or workshops which might be suitable for you.

These days, an excellent way to find out what's going on in your geographical area is to enter "BDSM" and the name of your nearest moderately-sized city into an Internet search engine. Many people mention where they are when they write about their own personal BDSM experiences online, and many social and support groups have an online presence as part of their own outreach programs.

The sorts of things you may find in your searches can include:

Education and support organizations - A number of groups, mostly organised by volunteers, provide training, seminars, websites, outreach programs, and newsletters both for people just getting into BDSM, and for people wanting to improve their BDSM skills. These can be great places to go for advice and other information.

Some of these groups can be quite large, some even having multiple locations spread across a number of states. A few to look at are:

- The Society of Janus (http://soj.org/)

- The Eulenspiegel Society (http://www.tes.org/)

- Masters And slaves Together (MAsT) (http://mast.net/)

Munches - These are regular social events often held in public cafes, restaurants, or coffee shops, where BDSM folk meet and chat. Munches are a good choice for your first steps into the BDSM world. You can go to munches anonymously and there's no ongoing commitment or expectation from you. If you like the people, you can keep going back until you're comfortable and ready to take the next step; namely, to start exploring BDSM with people you now know, but in a private atmosphere.

Workshops - These are organised training events where you can learn BDSM skills and techniques—such as how to safely tie someone up, or how to do fire play, or how to do flogging. If you're more into having these things done to you, go along and volunteer for people to practice on you.

Play parties - These are also social events, but are typically behind closed doors in premises containing well-equipped dungeons or play spaces. Play parties are opportunities for individuals and couples to meet up and engage in light and not-so-light BDSM activities in a social environment.

One of the advantages of play parties for newcomers is that there are always other people around. Most play-party organisers don't allow play to go on behind closed doors, and they ensure that there are experienced dungeon monitors keeping an eye on things. Playing alone with someone you've only just met can be risky, so a play party can be a good choice for your early outings. If you already know a few people from attending munches or workshops, then play parties can be safe and comfortable places to get your feet wet.

3.1 Precautions

When you think you have found a potential relationship partner and decide to get to know them better, arrange a safe call the first few times you're on your own with them, particularly if you're planning to do some BDSM play with this new person. A safe call is where you arrange to telephone a friend at a particular time to let them know that things have gone OK. Typically you give your friend the name of the person you'll be with, where you'll be, what you'll be doing, and when to expect a call from you. Your friend is supposed to call the police if they don't hear from you. You can't really be sure the first few times you meet up with someone new that they aren't Jack The Ripper, and letting them know that you've arranged a safe call can help keep you secure.

Don't be afraid to ask for references before you go off with someone, regardless of whether they're dominant or submissive, top or bottom. Talk to their previous partners and to others in your local community to see what sort of reputation they have.

If you're new to BDSM and are a submissive, ask around at munches and workshops to see if there are any more-experienced submissives who are happy to give you advice. Many larger support and outreach groups have mentoring programs where you can find someone who'll help you get to know the ropes [pun intended].

The same applies for new dominants. Playing safely can mean getting guidance on some of the more subtle points from people who have more experience than you. Don't be afraid to ask for demonstrations. Be polite though. If you're at a play party or workshop and see someone doing something interesting or new, ask them about it when they're free. Many dominants and submissives are proud of their skills and will happily share their knowledge and expertise.

3.2   Promoting yourself

If there are no opportunities to meet other BDSM folk near you, and there don't seem to be any people in your social circle who might be inclined to explore BDSM with you, then looking online for a partner may be a good option.

There are a number of websites where you can promote yourself and get known. At the time of writing two of the most active seem to be:

- Alt.com (http://alt.com/)

- FetLife (http://www.fetlife.com/)

When you do choose to make yourself known online, or when you look around online to see if there are any potential partners for you out there, here are a few things to keep in mind:

- You are trying to promote yourself so that you appear interesting enough to get to know. When you write about yourself, give yourself some depth. A one- or two-line summary of yourself is unlikely to attract anyone.

There are a lot of people who will write biographical information about themselves or describe their interests solely in terms of, "I need to serve you, mistress!" or "I am desperately in need of discipline!" While this makes it sound like all they want to do is take, take, take, it isn't necessarily a bad thing because there are folk out there who are really only interested in whaling into someone with a flogger. However, if you just want a severe caning, say so. If you just want sex, say so. The important thing is to be honest about it. If you want more than these things, include some personal information about yourself which makes it clear you're not just a life-support system for your cock or cunt.

- Don't include pictures of your genitals if you're serious about finding a relationship. On the other hand, if you want people to think of you as a dick or a cunt, then include pictures of your genitals by all means.

- Join online discussion groups whose topics are things you're interested in. Read what people are saying and add your thoughts. Avoid contributing comments that consist entirely of, "Me, too."

- Don't contact people privately without their permission. You'll seem like a stalker if you do.

- If you do find someone online who sounds interesting and you'd like to meet them face-to-face, ask for references and arrange a safe call. It's not very good if you drive to a secluded hotel in another state and find that this person is actually about fifty years older than they claimed online, or that they're armed with piano wire or an axe. Maybe meet in a coffee shop first.

3.3 Discussion

One of the big challenges to meeting other BDSM folk and finding potential partners is that BDSM is so often hidden away. In some of the more enlightened countries and cities of the world, BDSM and alternate sexualities are readily embraced. In other communities, even hearing about BDSM at all can be a rare event.

When you're new to BDSM, take the time to ask around, inform yourself about what options are available in your neck of the woods, and then get to know a few people before diving in to your first bondage, flogging, or other BDSM scenes. Even if it takes you well out of your way, when there are social events, workshops, or discussion groups anywhere near you, go along and join in. It is well worth your while.

Chapter 4

Build your own partner

Because there are so many different types of submissive, and because there are so many different types of dominant, getting yourself a partner can be very hard.

One of the first problems will be finding someone who is interested in the same activities as you. For example, you might be strongly attracted to bondage and all the people you meet might already have a well-developed interest in flogging, needle play, or something that you're not interested in at all.

A second problem is that the people you meet who already have some experience with BDSM might already be far more skilled or knowledgeable than you. They may not be able to, or may not be interested in, helping you to catch up to them.

One solution to finding a suitable BDSM partner is to make your own. You start out with someone who you like and who seems mostly compatible with you, and then you gradually introduce them to BDSM and see how they react. This could be someone you meet at work, at the supermarket, at a nightclub, or when out socialising with other friends.

While there are many aspects of BDSM which can be very scary and intimidating if you're suddenly confronted with them, there are many other BDSM activities which can seem interesting or fun, or just offbeat or kinky to newcomers. You can fairly safely introduce a new partner to them without having to worry that they'll think you're an axe-murderer and run away screaming. With any luck, once you've introduced BDSM to this new partner you may find that they readily embrace BDSM and are more than happy to explore it with you.

The question then is: how do you do this?

One strategy is that once you both are comfortable being alone together, invite them around to your home one weekend or evening. Then leave a well-illustrated—but not too extreme or explicit—practical guide to BDSM[1] either on your coffee table or somewhere else where they'll find it. Give them a chance to notice it and to maybe flip through it while you make coffee or while you prepare lunch or dinner.

When you know they've seen it, make a comment like, "I see you've noticed the book by Midori (or whoever). I was flipping through it the other day, and some of the things look like interesting things to try." See what they say.

---

[1] A couple of examples could be Midori's *The Seductive Art Of Japanese Bondage*, or Miller and Devon's *Screw The Roses, Send Me The Thorns*. These are both large-format books and are relatively innocuous. They should only scare away the hopelessly conservative.

Build your own partner

If you have reached the point in your relationship with this person where being naked and sweaty is not unusual, then another idea is to leave a few BDSM items lying around the bedroom and see how they react. I'd advise you to keep the scary stuff—such as your cage with the spikes on the inside, your whips, and your canes—locked away to start with, and maybe instead just leave some candles, a small pair of nipple clamps, and ONE short length of rope where your new partner can notice them.

Candles can be a gentle introduction into the sensation-play side of BDSM. Dripping a few warm drops of molten wax from a candle on the small of your partner's back can be quite sensual instead of scary or intimidating. Remember that you're trying to get them interested in BDSM. You don't want to overwhelm them and scare them away.

Another idea is to invite your potential new partner around to watch a carefully-selected movie and see how they respond to it. In particular, you want to see if they sit through it all the way, or if instead they find it so unappealing that they volunteer to wash the dishes, de-weed the garden, or re-grout the bathroom tiles while you watch the movie on your own. A positive sign is if, part way through, they start ripping off your clothes and grabbing at your crotch... We can only hope!

Here are a few movies with a distinctive BDSM flavour:

- *The Story of O* from 1975. Of course, this is a classic,

- *Secretary*. This is the 2002 movie of office perversion with James Spader and Maggie Gyllenhaal,

- *The Night Porter*, from 1974, with Dirk Bogarde and Charlotte Rampling.

Finally, and again if you've been hot and sweaty with this person, and if there's a conveniently-timed sex fair or exposition in your city, I suggest that you go along and make a point of being obviously very interested in the BDSM stalls and exhibits.

4.1 Conclusion

BDSM can be very scary and confronting. Taking someone who has no experience with BDSM to a play party where they see people flogged or whipped with blood running down their back, or where they see someone having large-gauge hypodermic needles thrust through their nipples, or where they see someone being dangled upside down by their testicles, is probably not going to help your chances of ever seeing them again.

On the other hand, showing them the sensual side of BDSM, or introducing them to something exciting but not too scary—such as blindfolding them, or tying just their wrists together—may get them interested. It also may turn out that what works for them is doing these things to you. You may find that that asking them to blindfold you, or to tie you up may be all that you need to start something powerful.

Picking the activities to suggest at this delicate stage of your relationship can be helped by coming up with your own list of things which: a) you'd like to explore with this new partner and, b) won't be too scary or confronting for them the first time around. In chapter 8, *The lists*, I have lists of many BDSM activities. Check them out. Maybe discuss some of them with your partner.

Build your own partner

Chapter 5

Criteria

When you're assessing someone new to determine what chance they have of being *the one*, you need criteria to measure them against. It's easy to meet someone at a BDSM party or social event and be carried away by their appearance or by their behaviour. Sometimes these outward signs can trigger deep and powerful responses in us. Are these a reliable guide to future contentment? Probably not, however they may still indicate that this person is worth a closer look.

When you meet someone and decide to give them a closer look, what sort of criteria or characteristics do you look for when evaluating them? Permanent and semi-permanent characteristics are things about them which either aren't going to change, which are going to change very slowly, or which they aren't going to lose. These are good characteristics to examine. For example, their intelligence is not going to change much over the course of their lives—at least, not until they're very old or they suffer some form of brain damage. Intelligence can be an important criteria when you are someone who likes to be mentally dominated. You aren't going to be satisfied by someone who is not able to be smarter than you.

Temporary or transient characteristics are things which are going to change, develop, or deteriorate in the short-term. These aren't going to be good criteria for considering long-term possibilities with someone. A top might have very poor mummification skills when you meet them, but a month later they may have attended an intensive workshop and now are pretty much an expert at it. Assessing them on something like this which can change quickly is not a good idea. On the other hand, if you're keen to do a mummification scene straight away then you clearly want someone who knows how to do it today, not someone who may know how to do it in a month.

Let's have a quick look at some of the most important permanent characteristics:

- **Intelligence** - how well someone can use their mind is something that is generally built-in. I'm not just talking about IQ here, but also how enthusiastically and how well someone will use their brain. If a potential partner is not too bright, or they are bright but won't use it, then that leaves the thinking to you. This may or may not be what you want. Alternatively, if they are bright and know how to use it then this could mean that either a very rich and challenging relationship is in store, or it could mean mental exhaustion.

- **Education** - what a person has learned through their lives is their education. It may be academic or may come from the school of hard knocks. Someone who is extremely well-educated may be a great choice if you're looking for intellectual stimulation or challenge, but may be overkill if you're looking for an uncomplicated life.

- **Skills** - being able to handle a relationship, and being able to engage in the sort of activities you want to explore is going to depend to some extent on the life skills, the interpersonal skills, and the BDSM technical skills of your partner. Some of these can be learned on the job, but knowing what sort of initial skill set you need your partner to have will make it easier for everyone.

- **Experience** - experience effects how well a person can make judgement calls. If you're looking for a constant and solid foundation for a relationship then go for lots of experience. If you're young, or if you're inexperienced yourself, or if you're looking to learn and grow with your new partner, picking someone with too much experience can be a liability because they've got less reason to grow and you're going to end up doing the growing all on your own.

- **Values** - these are what a person uses to make their judgements and decisions. They can include religious beliefs, family values, professional attitude, and so on. These values are generally learned at an early age and develop and mature as the person grows. Values show up in someone's sense of honour, their morality, and their ethics.

- **Emotions** - the importance of a person's emotions—how well they can express them, how deeply they feel, and how well they empathise—is going to govern the emotional depth or the emotional one-sidedness of a relationship with them.

You can usually get some idea of a potential partner's intelligence and education by talking to them. You can ask them questions about their background, mention things which are of interest to you and see if they can say something interesting back, see what interests them, and even ask them about school and university.

You can get an idea about their skills and experience often just by watching. Pick the sorts of skills and experience you're interested in so you can zoom in on them. Don't limit this just to what happens in the dungeon or bedroom. Life goes on outside of the dungeon and if you're looking for a long-term partner you need them to have other people-related and life-related skills. If they still live with their mother, for example, maybe they need some more life skills before you invest much time in them.

Values and emotions are harder to divine, and you probably need to spend more time with this potential partner to judge these. However, if they've passed your intelligence, education, skills, and experience assessments with flying colours then perhaps you can afford to get a little closer to them.

The opposite of permanent characteristics are temporary or transient characteristics. These are going to change over time, often quite quickly. Judging a potential partner on things which, by their very nature, come and go is likely to lead you either to reject perfectly suitable people, or to shack up with duds.

- **Situations** - the job someone has, how much money they have, and where they live all can change at the drop of a hat. Selecting a partner on the basis of how much money they have is, of course, shallow, but choosing someone because of their job or the suburb in which they live is not much better because these can easily change.

- **Relationships** - who your potential partner knows, who their friends are, and who they spend time with may be fascinating—particularly if they hang out with famous BDSM mistresses, awesome BDSM authors, rock stars, models, TV stars, or famous nobodies—but deciding that they'll be a good partner on the basis of these is a great way to end up with a hollow, and probably quite short, relationship. By all means check out the sort of person they like to be associated with, but the actual people shouldn't be something you judge them on.

- **Possessions** - and finally, one of the worst things to judge someone on is their possessions. Dungeons come and go, fancy floggers get lost or fall to bits, and latex undergarments get old and worn. Judge a potential partner on what and who they are, not what they own or have.

The most important way of distinguishing between the characteristics which will tell you what a potential partner will be like in a longer-term relationship is by looking at what they are, i.e., permanent characteristics, rather than what they have, i.e., temporary characteristics.

Chapter 6

Motivations

No one does BDSM or has a BDSM relationship for just one reason. There are always combinations of wants and needs involved, and before we can explore issues of relationships and compatibility we first need to understand our own wants and needs and those of our partners. For us to find our time with our partners satisfying and rewarding, be it for a quick scene or for a long-term relationship, we both must have our wants or needs met. If this doesn't happen, or it doesn't happen enough, then one or both of us will find our time together unsatisfying.

This chapter is a catalogue of reasons why people explore BDSM with a partner. You can read through it to help you identify what drives you and what drives your partner. It's not always obvious why we do BDSM and why we might prefer different activities and interactions with our partners at different times, but this chapter should help you nail down at least some of the things which drive you both. Armed with this information, you'll be better able to zoom in on the right things to do as the needs of you and your partner ebb and flow.

Ideally, you should go through this chapter with your partner. Importantly, be honest with yourself and with your partner as you do. BDSM isn't always socially or even emotionally acceptable and because of this you or your partner may not have even considered some of the things here as possible motivations. For example, if you like being tied up you may think that it's just because you like the feel of the rope. However, you may also have something inside you which hungers for physical surrender to the control of your partner. Liking the feel of the rope may be entirely true, but this could be a reason which is emotionally easier to swallow than admitting that you like being under the control of your partner.

When you don't know or don't admit to all the motives involved in your BDSM exploration, activities, and relationships, it makes it impossible to explore the full psychological and emotional intensity that's possible for you. In the rope example in the previous paragraph, if all you'll admit to your partner is that you like the feel of the rope when you actually want to feel them manhandling you, then when they're trying to do the right thing for you they'll be focussing on making the rope feel good. This is not what you really want. Instead, what you really want is for them to be more physical with you, but they're not going to do this because you haven't admitted this desire to them. Something similar applies when you are a top, dominant, or master: if you are hungering to feel your submissive writhing in agony on the ground as you torture them mercilessly, and all you say is that you want to give them a hard fucking, then what you'll get is only distantly related to what you really need.

Some of the wants or needs which are met by BDSM can be found in anyone—be they top, dominant, or master, or be they bottom, submissive, or slave. Often it's the case that these wants or needs are common to all humanity and that BDSM is merely particularly well placed to meet them.

Perhaps the main thing here is that BDSM often creates a context where the socially unacceptable becomes possible and even welcome. Where outside the dungeon such thoughts as hurting, humiliating, or objectifying someone are things you'd absolutely not mention to anyone for fear of getting locked away, in the world of BDSM they are things we can readily contemplate and discuss both with our partners and with our peers. Whether we do them or not is another matter. Just as we're free to talk about them, we are also free to do them... or not.

With that in mind, let's start out with a look at things which BDSM permits and which may be of interest to tops, bottoms, dominants, submissives, masters or slaves.

6.1   BDSM for quiet times

Although it might not seem like the highest-purpose reason for doing BDSM, when things are a little quiet around the house spending a bit of time in the dungeon with some rope can be an excellent alternative to TV. In this book I'm talking about BDSM relationships, and that means engaging your partner. Even if it's just some basic knot practice to fill in a quiet afternoon, doing these things together helps reinforce and develop your relationship with your partner.

Quiet times are also low-pressure times. If you're not trying to set a new record for pain tolerance or for the maximum number of knots tied on a single person at the one time, it means that you have time to muck about, try goofy things, and just generally experiment. Nothing is lost if what you try doesn't work out.

6.2 The real you

Rebellion is typically an in-your-face way of claiming ownership of yourself. It's about loud statements, such as shaving off all your hair, getting facial piercings, or riding a Harley. The act of rebellion can be very satisfying and feel very fulfilling. And, indeed, when we're talking about being loud and individual just check out your nearest BDSM play party!

Part of the story of BDSM and why it's so attractive much of the time is that it allows us to be ourselves. Many things that people do, even in the privacy of their own homes, are influenced or governed by opinions which come from outside. Despite some people's attempts to make it look like it only involves shiny leather catsuits and lightweight floggers, BDSM is rarely socially acceptable and embracing BDSM into your life means making a big psychological step towards saying, "I am going to be me, and not what the world wants me to be."

If you're looking to give yourself over to a partner who will use you in any way they want and still respect you in the morning, then this is entirely possible in BDSM.

If you're keen to have an orgy of sensations, be penetrated in every available orifice, be tied tightly while all this is happening so your struggles don't interfere with the action, then this is possible—and common—in BDSM, too.

If you're keen to be part of a relationship where the modern stuffy attitude of equality for women cramps your style, then

BDSM can and does support a pairing where inequality is the order of the day.

Chapter 8 of this book, *The lists*, contains lists of many, many BDSM activities to help you find things which will work for you. In some circles, these lists might be called *purity tests* and are basically checklists of activities where you get a score based on the number of activities on the lists which you've tried. They could probably more accurately be called impurity tests because they are commonly used as a self-measure of how much you've been corrupted in such areas as BDSM or sex, e.g., by how many different sexual activities you've tried—anal sex, oral sex, sex in public, sex with a stranger, etc.

Having said that, BDSM purity checklists are actually quite useful. Many people—particularly newcomers to BDSM—have no idea of the extent of the activities which fall under the umbrella of BDSM. BDSM purity tests can provide an excellent source of ideas and I encourage you to seek them out and explore. Many times you'll find things listed which you may never have thought of but which may work wonderfully well for you.

The important thing is that you need to look honestly at the activities listed and consider which ones might be genuinely satisfying or rewarding for you or for your partner. Ideally, you should sit down with your partner as you go through these lists, discuss the activities, and talk about what turns you on or off about each one. Try not to be too quick to dismiss or move past activities which turn you off. Take a moment or two to think critically about your reaction and whether it really is the case that this particular activity is not for you.

BDSM is really about being you. When you look at the things you like about BDSM, the things you do, the things you'd like to do, and the things you don't do, think about how much they let you express what you really feel inside, and think about how your partner and your relationship with your partner fit into you being able to be you.

6.3   Validation

Some BDSM folk use BDSM as a tool to validate themselves. In front of someone else—i.e., their submissive, bottom, top, master, or peers at a BDSM party or social event—practising BDSM or exercising a BDSM relationship can be validating and can confirm this person's role or status in their own eyes, in the eyes of their partner, and in the eyes of their peers.

Coming out of the BDSM closet the first time and putting your BDSM interests on display AND having them be accepted by people who you think of as your peers and contemporaries can be a very powerful and important support for your identity. Being able to be yourself, talk about your interests, and have others share and discuss these same interests gets rid of a lot of doubts and uncertainty about whether you're crazy, strange, or whether you should be locked up.

6.4   Punishment

As a top, dominant, or master, it sometimes falls to you to discipline or punish your submissive partner. In the context of a long-term relationship, there are three important situations when this can occur:

1. It could be punishment in a D&s context where your partner has failed to perform some task or other, or where their behaviour hasn't achieved the standard you are looking for. In other words, this is real punishment being applied to motivate your partner to perform better.

2. It can be when your partner experiences feelings of guilt which are completely unrelated to you. These could be feelings stemming from their childhood, from some other part of their past, or from something they've done recently—such as inadvertently hurt someone. They may look to you to help them assuage those feelings. Even though they haven't disappointed you *per se*, you provide the uncomfortable or painful activity which they can then internally process as punishment and feel better and cleansed because of it.

3. They may have entrenched ideas about right and wrong from their upbringing which conflict with the way they live their life now. This conflict might have to do with their work, friendships, or even their BDSM proclivities, and can leave them with lingering feelings of being "bad". Your punishment helps them find or create an internal balance.

Note that what I'm talking about in the above is not play punishment. It's not about creating playful or fun excuses to give your partner a spanking. It's about real discipline.

Because we're talking about a real need—and one which generally requires a partner to impose—punishment and discipline can be a significant opportunity in relationship terms. It's often something which is quite intimate and personal to the person needing the punishment, and this can be very powerful to share with them.

We can distinguish between real discipline and real punishment on one hand, and play discipline and play punishment on the other. When you have a casual or playful relationship with your partner, you can use manufactured or forced infractions by your submissive to playfully justify a bit of spanking, flogging, or erotic play. The sorts of infractions I'm talking about can include:

- Not addressing you correctly,

- Being to slow to bring you coffee, and

- Not squirming enough when you tickle them.

Punishment can also be about creating an emotionally safe context in which to explore other activities, such as pain, confinement, or humiliation. As I've noted here and in other places, some people have trouble accepting their BDSM inclinations—possibly struggling with the idea of deliberately being submissive or dominant, or with the idea of wanting pain from or inflicting pain on a loved partner. If we mentally associate BDSM with punishment then we make it into something which we can justify by connecting it with our past, such as our time at school, and this means that the sometimes difficult idea of wanting or needing pain can be attached to the more acceptable context of discipline at school.

Recognising when you're doing BDSM to address a real need for discipline or punishment compared to other times when you're doing it just for play or for fun will help you and your partner to get the most out of what you do. If one of you is looking for a real discipline scenario and the other is just playing then it's not likely to work out completely satisfactorily for either of you.

That said, there's no reason that a punishment scene focusing on a particular need can't later flow into something different such as playful fun once the main need has been met. This is something you need to discuss with your partner.

6.5   Intellectual challenge

BDSM is often primal, with many activities deliberately intended to focus on primal or animalistic wants and needs. Heavy pain play and rough manhandling fall into this category. These sorts of scenes can be relatively short, sometimes less than 20 to 30 minutes.

When there's more time available, and when any animalistic or primal urges have been explored and satisfied, some BDSM folk use their time to create opportunities to intellectually challenge and to compete with each other. I've noted in other writings[1] that you don't find Scrabble™ or chess boards in dungeons because these games tend to be too cerebral and actually detract from a BDSM mindset, but some forms of intellectual challenge do fit in.

Predicament bondage[2], for example, is one such activity. For dominants and submissives, predicament bondage is a chance for a submissive to test her partner and feel reassuringly put in her place when her dominant "wins".

---

[1] [MASTERS2008, pp. 27 - 39]
[2] See page 40.

Some escapologist bottoms thrive on trying to devise ways to escape the ropes or chains their top uses on them. Their relationships can contain nightly challenges where the top tries to devise a novel form of restraint while the bottom might spend all night trying to get out of it.

In the D&s or M/s world, a master or dominant might give his partner seemingly conflicting orders, or give them tasks which involve some difficult elements of planning, or even give them commands which end up being impossible to perform. The exercise for the slave or submissive then becomes one of resolving the conflicts or solving the problems which their partner has created for them.

For example, a dominant might have given his submissive a standing order to always answer the telephone and take a message when he is away. Then, when he needs to go out briefly he might order his submissive to remain in a certain seat until he returns. A few minutes after he leaves, he rings up anonymously using his mobile telephone[3]. What is his submissive to do? She has seemingly conflicting orders. Should she simply stay seated and let the telephone ring? Should she get up and answer the telephone? Should she maybe try to drag her chair over to the phone without getting up? If she does get up and answer the telephone, what should she do when she hears her dominant's voice? This is a conundrum which her dominant has created, which she can feel intensely subject to, and which can be an intellectual, rather than primal, challenge to resolve (or not!).

Challenges provide excellent opportunities for a dominant to compel the surrender of their partner. In many cases in BDSM,

---

[3]Let's assume that the submissive can't see the telephone number of who is calling.

surrender comes just in a physical, sexual, or primal form. Intellectual challenges allow this surrender to be taken and experienced at a conscious, rational, and intellectual level as well. They add to the involvement of both partners and create vistas for experiences well beyond the bounds of a dungeon.

6.6 Controlling your partner

Many BDSM activities provide an opportunity to take control of your partner. While things like flogging, caning, and erotic denial can have other appeals as well, much of BDSM also involves some element of control over your partner. Just on its own this exercise of control and power can be intensely exciting and rewarding.

- Impact play allows you to use the sting of the whip or cane to make your partner move and writhe when and how you want. If you're using impact play to sexually arouse your partner then the targets you choose, such as nipples or genitals, the way you hit these targets, how often you hit them, and what you hit them with, all determine how fast and how strongly your partner gets turned on.

- Bondage involves restraining your partner in some way. It can include tying them up with rope—either freestanding or to some object or piece of furniture, shackling them or restraining them with chain, placing them in a cage, or mummifying them with something like Saran® wrap. In all cases, this restraint renders your partner under your control. You can do with them what you like.

- Erotic denial is a type of sexual BDSM where you sexually stimulate and arouse your partner, but then you don't let them achieve climax... or, at least, not when they want to. You can do this as part of bondage play when you restrain them in such a way that they can't move and their genitals are exposed. You're then free to use your hand, fingers, a vibrator, or any other implement to sexually turn them on, but you always stop or slow down when they're getting close to orgasm until they beg for it.

- Predicament bondage is a variation of normal bondage where you deliberately allow your partner some limited freedom of movement. However, the position you create for them is uncomfortable. The challenge or predicament for them is that every movement they try has a cost. For example, you might tie them in a standing position with one foot attached to a rope which loops over a pulley to the hair on their head. If they put their foot down so they're standing on both feet, the rope pulls tightly and even painfully on their hair. If they hold their foot up, their leg quickly gets tired. The exercise of control here is that you get to create challenges and problems for them, and each time they find a comfortable position you rearrange the ropes to create a new and harder puzzle for them.

- Dominance and submission (D&s) is less about having particular scenes of flogging, bondage, cutting, etc., and more about control over your partner on an ongoing basis. It involves taking charge of them, setting directions or goals for them, monitoring them, giving them tasks and duties, and ensuring they perform them. For some submissives this can include discipline and correction for tasks poorly performed.

The control in D&s is explicit and often quite focussed. The control can feel more concrete because of the deliberate intention of the dominant to assert control and of the submissive to surrender to it. While there may be control in scenes such as cutting, bondage, etc., control in these situations is not so focussed and, indeed, is often merely implicit. For dominants who hunger to feel control over their partners, going straight for the jugular, so to speak, and issuing orders and requiring obedience can be far more arousing and satisfying than the unfocussed beating around the bush of flogging (pun intended).

- Mind fucks are BDSM scenes where you create a situation which, to your partner, appears more frightening, confusing, or challenging than it really is. For example, scratching a cold, blunt blade across your blindfolded partner's skin at the same time you dribble a small amount of warm water on the scratch can lead them to think that you've cut them; or lighting a propane torch behind them where they can hear it, moving the torch near their skin so they feel the heat, and then applying an ice cube to their bare skin can make them think you have burned them with the torch. In both of these scenarios you are manipulating your partner's sensations or perceptions so that they experience fear or shock and react accordingly.

- Humiliation is an activity where you criticise, humiliate, or embarrass your partner to drum home that their feelings of self-worth or value lie in your hands. You can make them stand in the corner wearing a dunce's cap, have them parade naked in front of their friends, or eat from a dog bowl. You control and challenge their confidence in themselves.

- Service is where your partner makes themselves available to satisfy some or all wants or needs you might have. This can include serving you drinks, making your bed, sexual service, running errands for you, being available when you feel the urge to hurt them, and so on. You direct them, determine the tasks they are to perform, judge their competency, set performance standards, and apply correction.

- Cutting and piercing are where you use a knife, needles, or skewers to penetrate the skin of your partner. You can use your partner as a canvas on which you might create designs of incisions, blood, or needles, or you might use the pain you inflict to control the state of mind of your partner.

As you can see, there are many direct or indirect ways of controlling your partner through BDSM activities. One of the big advantages here is that with so much choice about things to do you can control the experience of control itself. How much your partner feels themselves to be under your control is something you can vary to accommodate both your own desires and their ability to tolerate or absorb it. For example, if you tie your partner firmly to a chair then they may well be at your mercy, but how intensely they feel that is then going to depend on what you do to them. If you just leave them there then, true, they are under your control but they may find it merely to be a pleasantly relaxing experience. If, however, you take the opportunity to attach tight clamps to their nipples or genitals then that same situation is transformed into one where both you and your partner feel the intensity of the control that you can and are exercising over them.

Even D&s, where control is quite explicit, can be light or intense depending on what you do with it. For example, sending your submissive out to do some shopping may seem quite light, but standing over them as they scrub the floor under your supervision can be quite intense.

6.7   Symbolism

Symbolism can play a big role in BDSM.

Symbols can make it easier to enter into an appropriate state of mind before a scene. Uniforms are good examples of these sorts of symbols. For some people uniforms can be a fetish, but for others they can represent an authority dynamic which they're trying to achieve. A dominant or top wearing a police uniform can epitomise authority and can be easier and more natural to submit to than the same dominant or top wearing a sarong or a pair of budgie-smugglers[4]. A submissive wearing either a French maid's outfit or nothing at all can find it easier to get in the right mood than one who is wearing their customary jeans. And a dominant may find it easier to get in the mood when their submissive is dressed appropriately than when they are dressed in, say, a power business suit or as a tradesperson. Indeed, a top, dominant, submissive, or bottom who puts on the right clothes or who sees their partner in the right clothes can already find themselves getting into the right state of mind before they even start doing anything with their partner.

In fact, just the wearing of the clothes can be a reward in itself because, as we've noted earlier, self expression can be

---

[4] Australian slang for tight-fitting men's swimwear.

a valuable outcome of BDSM. When a BDSM relationship or even just a BDSM scene allows someone to express themselves more fully—such as with a uniform, with slutty clothes, with no clothes, or while posturing with a flogger—then this is already positive.

External physical symbols can be just as effective. A dungeon, the smell of leather, floggers, rope, and other toys are common BDSM symbols and can set the mood very well.

In addition to clothes, actions and words can also be symbolic. A diminutive female dominant can often physically subdue her larger male submissive, not by actually overpowering him, but by using symbolic actions to which he readily surrenders. These might be grabbing him by the shoulder and pulling him downwards so that he kneels, pushing the back of his head forward so that he bows, or taking his leash—assuming that he is wearing one—and guiding him to where she wants him. It's clear that this submissive is physically capable of resisting her, but the actions she takes and the force she applies often don't need to be more than symbolic. He will typically surrender to her intent and to the force of her personality. The actual use she makes of her own strength symbolises these two things.

Masters and slaves also use symbols. A master rarely needs to actually apply force to compel obedience. It can be enough that he merely shows his intent to take control and backs it up with his own strength of purpose. A master who says, "Stand up!" to his slave can be just as surely taking control as if he were to grab his slave and haul him physically to his feet.

Often this use of symbols can be as effective, or more effective, than an arduous display of physical dominance during a scene. It's true that sometimes symbolic control or symbolic adoption of a role needs to be reinforced by actual use of power or control, but it isn't the case all the time. Some scenes and activities can be just symbols and reminders of what has gone on in the past, or what may happen again in the future, and this can be a subtle but reassuring reinforcement of the relationship you have with your partner.

Finally, symbols can also be the goal, rather than just being a way of getting there. Being able to wear leather, or being able to wield a flogger are signs of achievement, and wearing a collar can be a sign of commitment.

6.8 Being controlled

I won't bore you with statistics, but the numbers show that a lot of people—vanilla and otherwise—have intimate relationships with their partner precisely because they want to experience power from their partner[5]. A lot of BDSM is about power and control, and there are many ways in which this desire to be controlled can be satisfied in BDSM.

- Bondage in its various forms—ropes, cages, cuffs, etc.— provides ways that your partner can physically restrain and control you.

- Flogging, caning, and other forms of impact play provide ways for your partner to manipulate and control you through sensations and pain.

---

[5]If you are keen to see some numbers, refer to [MASTERS2008, pp. 135 - 139], [HILL1996], and [MESTON2007].

- Dominance and submission, and mastery and slavery, provide ways for your partner to take control of you through orders, creating rules of behaviour and standing orders, by determining what you wear and what you eat or drink, etc.

- Humiliation, mind fucks, and interrogation scenes provide opportunities for your partner to manipulate you psychologically or emotionally.

- Sensation play—with heat, cold, textures, and sensations—provides ways for your partner to manipulate your feelings and awareness through controlling or stimulating your senses, such as smell, touch, hearing, etc.

- Hypnosis provides an interesting way of going deeper into control of your mind than other BDSM techniques allow. Post-hypnotic suggestions (commands you follow after being woken up from the trance) can be effective at helping you experience the feeling of control being taken away from you.

All of these things can be explored with your partner, and it's useful when you are sensitive or responsive to being controlled, and when it's something you find rewarding or satisfying, to discuss all the options above, and any others you can think of, with your partner.

Control can appear in many forms. It can play itself out in a large range of different ways such as helplessness or surrender on your part, or by creating situations where you might resist but be overwhelmed by your partner, and so on.

6.9   Developing trust

Trust can be hard to earn and easy to lose.   It is an important prerequisite when we're talking about engagement and penetration because these require as few barriers and defences as possible. For someone to lower their defences and be penetrated, and to allow their partner to see and engage the real *them*, they need to feel safe. This, in turn, means that they need to trust their partner.

Trust develops with experience.   For your partner to trust you, they need to see you respond to difficult and challenging situations. If they only ever see you when the sun is shining, the sky is blue, and when the birds are singing happily in the trees, then they're not going to be able to trust that you'll be able to deal with things when the sky is cloudy, when the thunder starts rolling in, and when the birds have all buggered off to hide in the local church steeple out of fear of the impending lightning.

BDSM can be a tool to help develop trust because BDSM isn't always blue sky and sunshine.   Many BDSM activities are challenging, and because there is often a risk of at least minor physical or emotional dents when penetration goes awry—such as when a flogger stroke hits in the wrong place, when a rope is too tight, when you or your partner experience an unexpected emotional reaction, or when a poorly-conceived order misfires—there are many more opportunities for trust to grow than there are in less confrontational activities such as a visit to the zoo or stamp collecting.

BDSM demands openness and honesty for penetration and engagement to occur.   Instead of trust developing incidentally as the people get to know each other, it is something which we should actively work towards because the more trust there is, the more powerful, penetrating, and engaging our BDSM will be.

I'm not talking about some magical quality of BDSM in any of this. Both you and your partner have more to gain or lose as far as trust is concerned than in a vanilla relationship. BDSM requires much more admitting to, and being open about, our intimate wants and needs. Sometimes these are hard to talk about and this makes the sharing and opening up very precious. Many BDSM activities, such as cutting and bondage, inherently require a lot of confidence in the skill and good intentions of your partner—certainly far more than you'd look for in vanilla-land.

When used with caution, BDSM can help you find someone who you can trust with your most valuable of possessions—your body and your soul.

6.10   Minimising self

There are people for whom the here-and-now nature of BDSM is the key to their interest in it. In the outside world they may be high-powered, thrive-under-pressure individuals who are driven to be in control of themselves and what's going on around them. This level of mental activity can be very hard to turn off. For these sorts of people unwinding and relaxing is a major enterprise. For them a hypodermic needle tip through the genitals or pulsing electric shocks through the nipples can compel a change of focus far more effectively than sitting down in front of the television and watching a rerun of Magnum P.I., going for a run along the beach, or doing a workout at the gym.

Some forms of BDSM absolutely require a surrender to the experience and force a change of focus. This is something that is difficult to find outside of BDSM, at least in ordinary circumstances, but it's also something that's often vital when you want to turn off and simply be.

Some BDSM activities merely give you the opportunity to focus on them. Rope bondage is a good example. If there's enough stress or worry outside the dungeon it can intrude on your experience under the rope. You can even be distracted by loud noises or a song on the radio. If, on the other hand, you have hypodermic needles being inserted through your testicles or clitoris then you might not even notice a meteorite strike.

The intensity of such forms of BDSM takes a complex man or women and reduces them to their basics. It pushes aside the civilised layers of behaviour they have learned and which they are required to wear outside the dungeon and strips them down to their bare self. It compels surrender and creates a form of tranquillity. This is a very powerful result of BDSM. It is not recreation or an escape from the worries of the external world, but is instead an escape from self.

Some of the BDSM activities which can compel this sort of outcome include:

- Piercing - using hypodermic needle tips, sewing needles, or skewers to penetrate a part of the body such as nipples, belly, back, or genitals. While this might outwardly look decorative or be a way to create designs using patterns of needles, the psychological effect can often be quite profound.

- Cutting - using a sharp, sterile knife to cut into the upper arms, chest, breasts, back, or belly. Again, this can outwardly be to create designs in the flesh, but the cutting often causes intense and inescapable pain. For some people, the sight of their own blood can also be overwhelming.

- Flogging - using multi-tail floggers to create either intense stinging or heavy thudding sensations. Some floggers and how they're used can create very strong scoring or cutting sensations, while others can be heavy and pounding and their thuds resonate through the whole body.

- Mind fucks - manipulating your partner's experience so they think something intense or dangerous is happening to them when in reality they are quite safe. Triggering a fear of falling or a fear of the unknown while your submissive is blindfolded can also be quite terrifying.

If it seems that I'm talking about something which might be useful to you here, then discuss it with your partner and engage them in the search for activities which work for you.

Importantly, keep in mind that when you're looking for these sorts of intensities they tend to be very one-way things. That is, when you're lying face up having patterns carved into your breast, or when you're receiving a heavy flogging, it might be truly effective for you but it might just be work for your partner. They're there concentrating on making sure you get the pain or the intensity necessary to get you to the state of mind you need, and they're making sure you stay safe and healthy, don't die of blood loss, and so on. While they may be doing it because they care about you, be sure to make it up to them later in some way through BDSM scenes where you focus on getting their needs met, or by creating opportunities for them to do what they want.

Motivations

6.11   Be the canvas

For some people the draw of BDSM is not so much how the different BDSM activities affect them, but is instead about surrendering themselves for use by their partner.

Surrender can be an intense and powerful act.   It can be profoundly intimate, emotional and spiritual. For example, many tops and dominants use heavy scenes, such as floggings or canings, as a way to work out their own tensions or stresses. Their submissive partners may not have the need to work out their own stresses or tension at the time, but the experience of placing themselves at their partner's disposition and being heavily used, as well as the experience of meeting the demands of their partner's needs, can be very powerful and satisfying to someone who is inclined towards surrender and service.

Similarly, for someone who is not into being cut themselves *per se*, they may find that through making their body available to their partner for the cutting of designs in their flesh the surrender and service aspect becomes an intense and intimate time with their partner.   The same can apply when your partner enjoys creating piercing designs with hypodermics needle tips in your skin, or when they tie elaborate patterns of rope and knots all over your body to express themselves.

This surrender can be a form of objectification, making yourself into a tool or a canvas with which your partner expresses themselves.   Earlier I mentioned minimising self as a reason why some people do BDSM. Surrendering yourself to being the canvas on which your partner expresses their needs and desires can be another way of achieving this.   You reduce yourself to being nothing more than an object on which your partner works out their own needs.

6.12   Self ownership

Because BDSM is seen to be socially unacceptable in some quarters—particularly in the more conservative or fear-ridden parts of our society—actually getting involved in and embracing BDSM can be a loud and powerful statement about your identity. Instead of going with the flow or trying to conform to what society says you need to be, entering the world of BDSM is saying that you are your own man or woman and are setting your own path.

Also, some people come from backgrounds or situations where their family or social group disempowers them. Or, put another way, their family or social group applies pressure—sometimes irresistibly—to get them to behave in certain "acceptable" ways. Effectively their choices get made for them and they have no real control over their own lives. They get told what to do and are expected to do it. This can extend to the clothes they "choose" to wear and even to the job they "choose" to do. Sometimes this pressure is due to their cultural or ethnic background, but it can equally come from being born into a conservative family, or it can come from the church you attend, or it can come from the people with whom you hang out. It leads to you feeling like you don't have control over yourself or that you don't own yourself.

To counter this, engaging in activities which significantly affect your own body can make a powerful statement about ownership of yourself and can go part of the way to compensating for these feelings of powerlessness. Outside of BDSM, wearing weird clothes and getting a tattoo can be ways of compensating because they say and demonstrate that you can do what you want to yourself regardless of what other people tell you.

In terms of statements however, being involved in BDSM goes a whole lot further. For some people, just the symbolism of being a BDSM practitioner can be a powerful statement and an act of rebellion. The real BDSM itself can be merely icing on the cake.

There are a number of BDSM activities which let you get an intense feeling of ownership over yourself and which can give you a way of feeling that you're not under the control of parents and family, teachers, particular people in your peer group, or society at large. For example:

- Flogging and whipping are very symbolic in terms of ownership. Allowing someone such as your partner to flog or whip you is a powerful step in terms of deciding what can and can't be done to you. These are acts which directly enter your personal space and by allowing or requiring someone to do these things to you, you are saying that you are in control of who hurts you, who marks you, and who triggers deep feelings inside you.

- Cutting and piercing often make marks or patterns on your flesh. Allowing yourself to be used by your partner for the creation of patterns or designs on and in your skin, particularly if you have had a hand in the designs themselves, is another strong way to say that this is your body and that you decide what happens to it.

This problem of self-ownership doesn't just apply to bottoms, submissives or slaves. In many cases, folk who are naturally inclined towards being tops, dominants, masters, or mistresses feel themselves pressured to conform to other standards and can't let their natural desires see either the light of day or the dark of a dungeon.

For some people, being involved in BDSM is a reclamation of themselves. It can be a taking back of control of themselves and how they express themselves. This can have a particularly strong impact on how the person or people involved feel about themselves. If they are compelled to live their day-to-day lives as something they don't feel or aren't passionate about, then letting their hair down and being themselves in the privacy of their dungeon with their partner can be very reaffirming and build up a lot of self-confidence.

This is because BDSM creates its own unique context where you can be intense with your partner. It provides circumstances and activities where you can be far more passionate and even primal than street life allows. Society tells you to be calm and sedate and not to get worked up about anything. On the other hand, BDSM is about deep feelings and intensity. It often provides a way of taking back the control of your wants and needs which society tries to take away by telling you how to behave and what's good and what's not. BDSM instead encourages you to do many of the things society says are no-nos.

The important thing about self-ownership is that it is about boundaries. When the world around you has told you, possibly for your entire life, that there are things which you can't do to yourself, or that there are things that you can't change about yourself, then this creates a fundamental boundary line inside you which can be difficult or impossible to pass on your own. Crossing this boundary and properly claiming control over yourself is an act of rebellion just as much or more than getting a tattoo or wearing weird clothes. It can be a sign that you're stepping out of the shadows which have hidden you away both from yourself and from the rest of the world.

Your partner can be a significant part in this with you, and this is something you both can usefully explore together. While it's not limited to submissives, if you are submissively inclined then this is also an important part of your own journey because before you can give yourself to your dominant or master you need to own yourself fully to begin with.

6.13   Expiation of guilt

Another reason why people do BDSM is because it can have a discipline or punishment aspect. Some forms of impact play such as spanking, caning, and flogging are obvious examples of things which have an association with childhood discipline or punishment. Confinement, such as being locked in a cage or being compelled to sit in the corner, are others. This discipline aspect of BDSM becomes even more apparent when the people involved enact their punishment scenes in rooms decked out to look like schoolrooms, or when the one being punished dresses as a schoolboy or schoolgirl.

Spanking, flogging, and caning are great staples of BDSM. You'll find them in most places where BDSM is practised. Sometimes guilt is a motivator for doing them because some parts of our culture are very good at instilling guilt into people and it can last a very long time. If you're one of these people with such a burden, and you were repeatedly disciplined at school then perhaps something similar in a BDSM dungeon can provide a suitable context and help you to get the guilt out of your system.

BDSM can provide a safe, supportive environment in which this expelling or expiation of guilt can occur. But again, it's important that you communicate this need to your partner. A flogging for kinky sex is very different from a flogging for guilt, and when your partner knows exactly what you're looking for they can help make sure that you get the punishment you need.

6.14   Self harm

One of the uncomfortable truths about BDSM is that it isn't always sweetness and light. Some people might have you think that it's only about kinky sex or that it's just about a bit of fun in the bedroom. While this may sometimes be the case, there can also be a darker side.

Self harm is one of these darker sides, and one particular form of self harm sits well—or as well as such a thing can—with BDSM. This is cutting. It bears some outside similarity to the cutting we find in BDSM and it's particularly prevalent among young women. It involves using a blade or knife to cut or scratch oneself and cause sharp pain. The cuts can range from long shallow cuts to deeper cuts releasing possibly a lot of blood. People who cut in this way will almost always do it on their own, often in the bath or shower where the blood will easily wash away. They're needing the pain, and it's this pain which provides temporary relief from what ails them.

There are many reasons why people cut. It's outside of the scope of this book to explore why they cut, but the point is that they do. While you can argue that in an ideal world no one would have the need to cut themselves, our world is not ideal and for some people cutting is the best or only option they have.

Because the need to cut is often embarrassing or is something you don't talk about with others, you are likely to do it on your own. If you're in need of pain from cutting and the need is strong, you may cut too deep. Worst case scenario: if you cut too deep there may not be anyone in the house to help you and you could bleed out and die. And if you're cutting because you have an intense need to do so, you may not pay attention to some of the more fiddly bits of cutting such as using sterile blades and making sure your cuts don't get infected.

While BDSM can't get rid of the need to cut, it can provide an environment where it's much safer. If you do have this need for pain, then having your partner cut you instead of you cutting yourself provides a number of benefits—safety being the main one.

- By having your partner wield the blade instead of you yourself, it allows you to more fully surrender to the pain. When you are holding the blade and doing the cutting, part of you has to stay in control. With your partner taking care of both the blade and your well-being, you can just feel and sink into the pain.

- Your partner will not be under the influence of your strong need for pain and they'll be able to pay attention to practical matters such as making sure they don't cut too deeply, and ensuring that the cuts are kept clean and disinfected.

- You don't have to worry about being interrupted.

- Your partner can cut areas where you can't normally reach. Commonly, people who cut themselves will use their bellies, forearms, and thighs because these are easily reachable. Because of the scarring involved it means that they have to wear long sleeves, long pants, and can't go to the beach wearing a swimming costume. Your partner can cut areas you can't reach, such as your shoulders or your buttocks, so that other more public parts of your body (arms, legs, etc.) don't need to be covered up due to scarring.

It can be hard to admit to your partner that you have such a need for pain through being cut. It can be psychologically easier to tell everyone, including yourself, that you're into this aspect of BDSM for the kinky sex or that you're simply submitting to your partner as a canvas for their designs with a blade. However, if you don't admit your need to your partner then you reduce the chances that your need will get met. You may find that some cutting scenes with your oblivious partner are not enough and that you need to retreat into the shower or bath when the need is particularly strong and do more cutting yourself.

Try being open with your partner, and even if you feel that it's something that you shouldn't be doing but you need to do it anyway, tell them and maybe they'll be ready and willing to help you out with their skills.

6.15 Being touched

Touching is one of the most under-mentioned aspects of BDSM. Touching your partner—especially non-sexual touching—is a vital part of any close relationship. It helps create feelings of companionship, intimacy, and caring. When we communicate with our partners, a touch can easily signify as much or more than words alone.

In BDSM, the activities we do provide many opportunities for touching, but when we discuss these activities, go to workshops about them, or read about them in books, the fact that touching is involved is often not mentioned at all. If we don't touch each other during BDSM play, the play becomes very sterile or clinical. This might be fine for the occasional medical scene, but as part of a relationship we should be looking for times when we can physically touch or be touched by our partners, either intentionally or as an important incidental part of our play.

Some of the sorts of touching which can occur include:

- Squeezing

- Caressing

- Pinching

- Biting

- Licking

- Pushing

- Pulling and dragging

- Sucking

- Face slapping

- Back-handed slapping

- Tickling

- Spanking

- Kissing

- Poking

- Blowing

- Twisting nipples

- Brushing with your hand

- Brushing lightly with your hair

- Tying knots against bare skin

Some of these might seem more incidental than fundamental parts of play, but as you're reading this, think about the things you do with your partner. How do you feel when they touch you? How do you feel when you touch them? What would it be like if the touching was missing? Think about the difference between an open-handed spanking versus spanking with a paddle. Are they the same? Do they feel as intimate and close? What about nipple torture with clamps versus nipple pinching and twisting with fingers. Do you get the same feeling of connection?

It's worth noting that we can sometimes have too much touching, just as we can sometimes have too little touching. For someone who enjoys the tactile side of things and who finds the touch of their partner during play to be reassuring, this latter can certainly be the case. On the other hand, for someone who wants or needs to sink into the physical sensations their partner is inflicting on them—such as during cutting, nipple torture, flogging, or bondage—being touched too much can be a distraction.

If there are times during play when you want or need your partner to keep their hands off you, let them know when it's good to touch you and when it's a distraction. Many people find that being touched during heavy impact play or heavy pain play is a distraction, but being held, touched, or even just having their partner nearby when they are coming down from the experience

Motivations

can be the bee's knees. If this is the case with you, say so if your partner hasn't already worked it out.

Let's look in more detail at a few of the ways that touching enters into BDSM play:

- Nipple torture. Touch is pretty obvious here when you're pinching your partner's nipples between your fingers, but even when you're using nipple clamps there's incidental touching as you perhaps pull on your partner's nipple to stretch it out to make it easier to attach a clamp. You might also incidentally or on purpose caress their breast as you place the clamp.

- Flogging. While the flogging itself is a hands-off activity, it's common for a top to warm up their partner with a spanking; then, as the flogging progresses, to check how their partner is going from time to time by stopping and feeling the warmth of their skin. Maybe at the end of the scene they also poke and prod a bit to check for any bruising. All of this is, of course, incidental touching.

- Cutting and piercing. These both involve a lot of touching in the form of rubbing your partner's skin with antiseptic, pressing or stretching their skin prior to inserting the knife blade or needle, touching or pressing on wounds, applying dressings, and so on.

- Physical handling or manhandling. This is often a fairly robust activity involving grabbing part of your partner's body—such as the scruff of their neck, their throat, or their shoulders—and using a modicum of strength to push them around, press them against the wall or down on the bed, or push them down on to their knees. The main goal of this is the experience for both of you of strength and physical power. But don't underestimate the role of person-to-person touching in this. Being touched at the same time you're being manipulated by your partner can be quite powerful. Would it be the same if you used a rope to haul your partner around, or would it be the same if you were hauled around on a rope by your partner instead of having the actual physical touch?

- Bondage. The focus of bondage is often ropes, knots, and chains, but along the way there's often a lot of physical touching or brushing of hands on skin as the ropes or chains are positioned. This may be quite an important part of what makes bondage work for you and your partner. Lack of touching can make bondage quite clinical and while this works for some people it's not always what is wanted or needed.

- Communication. BDSM is frequently deliciously primal. It addresses animal wants and needs, and these are best communicated physically. Grabbing someone and manhandling them, caressing them, slapping them, pinching them, and even fucking them, all communicate something via touch and physical sensation.

- Expressions of tenderness. Some BDSM is hard and heavy, but sometimes BDSM can be an expression of love or tenderness and this almost always involves some form of person-to-person touching. Light sensation play is an ideal opportunity for this, particularly when you're exploring tactile sensations with your partner. The goal needn't be pain, but do be sure to start and end the play with lots of stroking and touching.

- Reassurance. Actually being there, in physical contact with your partner, can be reassuring or comforting before, during, and after a scene. You sometimes don't even need to be particularly active about it. Just the contact with your partner or the pressure of one part of your body up against theirs can do the trick.

It's good to spend a little time talking about touch with your partner. Reflect on all of the BDSM activities you do together and think about when you touch each other. Could the experiences be improved by changing the nature of your touching and how much there is of it? Would more touching be better in, say, bondage and less in flogging? Or maybe the other way around? Or something different altogether?

6.16 Bonding

In terms of relationships, one of the most positive outcomes from practising BDSM is creating strong intimate and emotional bonds between partners. This bonding occurs for a number of reasons:

- More so than in vanilla relationships, successful BDSM requires openness and honesty. If you don't admit to your secret needs and desires then your partner will never know the sorts of things which are most important and satisfying to you.

  Because of this, people into BDSM need to, and do, talk to each other about important and intimate things more than their vanilla counterparts. This sharing of our intimate selves removes barriers between us and makes bonding more likely to occur.

- BDSM also allows for more intense psychological, emotional, and physical experiences with your partner. For many folk, BDSM is about affecting their partner, about causing them to feel and respond in intense ways. The feeling of being entered or penetrated by your partner—even when not sexually, such as through pain, needles, or knives—is something you don't get with the non-BDSM people in your life and this can create tight bonds between you and your partner.

- Much of BDSM is about power and control, and to fully get the benefit and to fully respond to what's happening between you and your partner, you need to open yourself up. More than just talking and saying what rocks your boat, you need to expose your intimate self to your partner and you need to allow them to affect you. This can be both very powerful and, at the same time, empowering as you let them in to touch and trigger you.

  While it might sound like this is just what a submissive feels while they are receiving attention from their dominant, it actually works both ways. A dominant also needs to be open to how you respond, what you say, how you react, and how you feel. They also need to have reactions and feelings which are going to be triggered by you. They need to surrender to the possibilities of their own feelings and feel safe doing so with you.

- On a more mundane note, intimacy also can also come from the exploration and exploitation of some very private parts of your anatomy—and not just your clitoris, breasts,

Motivations

or penis. BDSM can leave no stone unturned in its exploration of your body. Privacy is something you need to be ready to surrender, and accept that all of you is fair game.

You may feel an intense closeness with your partner when they are completely at your mercy—perhaps when they're tied and helpless, or while you are using potentially dangerous implements on them, such as knives or whips. This show of trust on their part can be something which helps bring the two of you closer together.

If this aspect of BDSM is important for you and your partner, make sure that you create opportunities from time to time to actually explore and savour this. While other BDSM activities may also be exciting in their own ways and for their own reasons, bonding and closeness can be entirely valid, and even highly important, outcomes for an evening's or weekend's BDSM explorations.

6.17 Recreation and fun

Day-to-day life can be full-on, stressful, and overwhelming. It can take your mind away from happy thoughts, and even after you've finished work for the day it can leave you thinking about challenges at work, about problematic situations with co-workers or family, and about difficult decisions that need to be made. By spending an hour or three in the dungeon with your sweetie, aided by some ropes, some candles, and an array of other bits and pieces, you and your partner can flee into a BDSM world where everything outside no longer matters and is no longer relevant. This is a great way to escape and to relax.

The point of this is to unwind, to retreat into your dungeon or play space and have a seriously good time with your partner. Remember that BDSM doesn't always need to be intense. BDSM scenes can be times to play. Fun can be a necessary part of a relationship, and you sometimes need to ensure that there are opportunities for it between you and your partner. A lack of fun can have a big impact on the success of your relationship.

Fun and recreation as goals can almost be in direct contrast to satisfying animalistic hungers and passions. However, remember that fun can lead to other things which may be more primal, and just because you entered the dungeon with light fun in mind doesn't mean you can't finish up with something heavy and intense if it feels right to do so.

Indeed, for those of you who have difficulty putting your worries aside as you enter the dungeon, some serious attention with a flogger or with some needles is sure to drive other thoughts out of your mind and just leave you with the immediacy of what is happening between you and your partner *right now*.

Fun and recreation are often about distracting you from your everyday life and BDSM can be entirely suitable for achieving this goal. The vast majority of BDSM activities involve things quite unlike the outside world. Whether you're on the receiving end of drops of hot wax, or whether you're the one doing the dripping; or whether you are being tied with so much rope that you could be mistaken for a giant ball of string, or whether you're the one doing the tying; or whether your partner is carving their initials into your upper arm with a scalpel, or whether you're the one doing the carving; or whether you're focussing on getting your pony trot just right, the fact is that there's a lot of focussing on the here-and-now going on and this will certainly drive other thoughts away.

Motivations

In it's own way it is relaxing, and at the end of an undistracted BDSM session both people involved can feel very relieved. They can unwind. Tension dissipates and you are left feeling cleansed.

If any of this sounds good to you, tell your partner. Some people mistakenly think that each BDSM session needs to be heavy or full-on. This isn't the case. If using BDSM for relaxation or fun some or all of the time is what works for you, pursue it with your partner. Even if you have no specific BDSM activity in mind, just going into your dungeon with the idea of being open and trying new things can be a good way to have fun.

There's a difference between this BDSM for recreation and fun and the BDSM for minimising self which I talked about earlier[6]. Using BDSM for recreation is about getting yourself into the here-and-now and pushing distracting thoughts aside. The end result is you totally focussed on what's happening.

Minimising self, on the other hand, is about actually diminishing yourself, making yourself less. It is about escaping from yourself for a short time and so while the lights may be on, so to speak, you're actually not at home.

6.18   Primal expression

BDSM activities and relationships provide opportunities to express ourselves primally and to get primal needs met.

A lot of the time when I talk about primal needs and primal expression I would be talking about things like physical handling and aggression, and about sex. But primal also relates to:

---

[6]In section 6.10 on page 48.

- Fear,

- Strong and deep emotions,

- Food, hunger, and thirst, and

- Social needs (i.e., being with and interacting with others)

All of these things are part of us, and when they become part of our BDSM and of our BDSM relationships we can have a powerful context in which to address them and to find release and satisfaction.

For example, our social needs can be met with fellow BDSM enthusiasts. Not just with our primary BDSM partner, but also with others who we maybe meet at BDSM play parties or at social BDSM get-togethers.

Perhaps there's a reason why formal dinners prepared and served by BDSM slaves are a real goal for some and a fantasy for others. The ideas and images of mastery and slavery aren't of sandwiches while watching the news on TV, but instead are of sumptuous, multi-course meals on long tables with candelabras. The image is normally of a feast or meal with a number of others present, some serving and some being served. Note the social context of this, i.e., it's a formal occasion for social interaction.

The need to express ourselves physically can come through heavy manhandling during BDSM play or through rough sex. Two of the three criteria I mentioned in book one for a BDSM relationship—namely, penetration and disparity of power—are clearly present here.

One of the reasons why primal expression is particularly relevant to BDSM is that our oh-so-proper society doesn't provide much opportunity or encouragement for expressing the animalistic or primal side of our natures. We sometimes have the chance to get a little bit of vicarious excitement at football games or while watching demolition derbies, but the rest of the time when we're with other people the rules say we need to be quiet, respectful of others, not to be bossy, to be sedate, calm, not to speak loudly, etc., etc. This is a bit of a bummer because we humans are animals and it wasn't too long ago that we were whacking each other with clubs as foreplay. We certainly haven't outgrown our built-in inclinations towards being physical.

Notwithstanding some of the vigorous rumpy pumpy which goes on in some households, sex itself—one of the few really primal things many people actually get to do—is often wrapped in guilt. Some quarters of society tell us it should only be done to make babies, or that it should not involve bruises or blood loss, or that it should only be quiet and gentle. Sex in perfumed rooms on silk sheets might be romantic, but it doesn't necessarily satisfy the animal inside. Embracing BDSM is one way to open the gates to powerful, immensely satisfying, and very animalistic self-expression.

A funny thing about the missionary position is that it quite literally involves one person pinning their partner down. Expressed like that, it is beginning to sound BDSM-ish. Even women not into BDSM report that the feeling of being pressed under their partner is a powerful, exciting, and desirable experience, but in missionary position sex this can be more incidental than intentional. In fact, some people engage in sex because it's one of the few socially acceptable ways for them to be physically dominated or to physically dominate someone.

Through BDSM however, you can make strength, power, and domination a planned and agreed part of what goes on in the bedroom or dungeon, and this can help make previously guilty pleasures into the main event.

Some parts of BDSM are actually all about this, and so by including BDSM in your life you get the opportunity to express the animalistic parts of you in an open and honest engagement with your partner. And when the hungers for domination and submission which you and your partner feel are particularly strong, you may find that sometimes you won't even think about the sex part because the D&s side has been so rewarding in itself.

This physical, animalistic side of BDSM appears in some, but not all BDSM activities:

- Many tops who practise flogging will often have a range of floggers in their arsenal (sorry, toybag) ranging from the small and light floggers used more for sexual titillation—such as for flogging clitorii, testicles, or nipples—through to the heavy, pounding floggers which actually do start to trigger animalistic feelings and urges both for the person receiving the rough and heavy thuds, and for the person using all their strength to wield the flogger and strike their partner.

- Physical domination, including wrestling and manhandling, can also contribute mightily where animalistic urges and hungers are in play. The actual use of physical strength, both to subdue on one side, and to resist on the other, can be extremely powerful between two people. It can create intense feelings of dominating, overwhelming, and of compelling the surrender of your partner, or it can create feelings of complete helplessness and submission.

  We need to be cautious here because some styles of physical domination are merely symbolic or cooperative rather than actual, particularly where the dominant is a small female and the submissive is a large male. Symbolic or cooperative physical domination will be far less satisfying in a primal sense than actual physical domination.

- Bondage, another very common BDSM activity, can be light-and-fluffy or heavy and intrusive. Just being tied to a chair is not likely to be very useful in terms of satisfying animal urges, but bondage involving lots of heavy handling and the opportunity or even need to resist can be very effective.

If this talk of primal passions, animal feelings, being rough, or physical manhandling triggers something inside you, you should discuss it with your partner if you haven't already. There is a strong tendency in many people, particularly in newcomers to BDSM, to not be rough or heavy because society teaches us that this is a "bad thing"... and sometimes it can be. However, many people are drawn to activities like bondage or flogging because of the possibility that a few knots may lead to some physical handling or that light flogger taps may evolve into some serious pounding. Indeed, they may hunger for this primal physicality but be uncomfortable asking for it because they might think it's wrong—such as for a big, tough dominant to forcefully take physical advantage of their small and petite partner—but this may be exactly what the doctor ordered.

Such explorations and activities need to be approached confidently, and this can only be done when you have full and open communication with your partner. Things can go badly astray when there are hints or promises of animalistic needs being explored and only a light tap of a flogger or a quick tie-up ensues, so you need to be clear about what you want or what you are prepared to do.

While I've been mainly focussing here on primal expression and feelings in the form of the use of physical strength this is only because this is one of the easiest and most accessible primal feelings which we can reach or activate through BDSM. As I mentioned at the start of this section, others things—such as food and sex—can be just as primal and should not be neglected.

6.19   Surrender

To fully and completely surrender to something can be a transformative experience. It means lowering all of your barriers and allowing something to enter you, or allowing yourself to experience something completely without resistance. Surrender differs from submission in that submission often simply means moving some—but not all—barriers aside temporarily and then putting them back when the scene or activity is done.

Surrender works to create change in the person who experiences it. This change might be a deeper understanding of self, a greater awareness of what you are capable of feeling, a more open attitude to what goes on around you, and perhaps more honesty and trust in regards to your partner.

Surrender is powerful and frequently very intense. Because it means opening yourself up, what happens to you while you are surrendered will often reach deeper inside you and affect you more strongly than when you simply submit to what's going on. Surrender is also sometimes hard to identify, but many people into BDSM are actually looking for it regardless of what specific activity they do.

Many BDSM activities compel surrender. That is to say that surrender is a requirement, not an option. This is because the activities themselves are so intense that they force barriers to come down. For example, strong pain play such as heavy flogging or caning can do this. Indeed, some people seek out heavy or intense BDSM activities precisely because they are looking for surrender and these sorts of scenes guarantee it. On the other hand, some sensation-based activities, such as wax play, may not get anywhere near intense enough to compel surrender and may be merely sensually pleasant or erotic.

Surrender is one of the most powerful and transformative experiences in BDSM, and yet it is also one of the one's least mentioned and least explored. But understanding surrender, and understanding how and where it fits into your life and into the lives of people around you, is a fairly critical factor in getting yourself into the sort of relationship which will be effective and satisfying for you.

One of the difficulties of coming to grips with BDSM relationships is that there are labels we use to describe ourselves which have differing meanings. These terms include:

- Top
- Bottom
- Dominant
- Submissive
- Master
- Mistress
- Slave

- Switch

The terms themselves have widely different meanings depending on who you ask, who they're with when you ask, where you ask, how you ask, which country or city you're in when you ask, the time of day when you ask, the weather conditions when you ask, and practically anything else you can think of. However, the terms do hint at the place surrender has for that person.

Surrender is not submission. While they may look the same on the outside, surrender is more profound than submission. It is the process by which we open ourselves to an experience and allow it to enter into us completely and without resistance. There is an air of helplessness to surrender because it means that we must open the door and completely step out of the way.

Submission, on the other hand, is frequently just acceptance or tolerance. We can see this where bottoms and submissives retain the option of saying no; whether this is no to continuing a scene, no to getting a drink for their dominant, no to dressing in a particular way, no to their partner's wish that they fuck someone else, or no to anything in general that their partner would like. In submission, you stand at the door ready to close it at any time.

In reality, there are many doors. A submissive or bottom may have one door that they keep open all the time for bondage experiences, another that they open occasionally for personal service to particular partners, one that they keep firmly closed for anal sex with strangers, yet another which they open from time to time for cutting scenes, and so on.

We can call BDSM slaves the people who seek to surrender as much as possible to their partner. Continuing the door analogy, a slave seeks to step away from their doors, or from as many of their doors as possible, and let their partner—their master—completely and unreservedly control the doors instead.

6.20   Catharsis

Emotions and nervous energy sometimes build up during the course of our lives. This often happens when we don't have the opportunity to safely get these emotions or this energy out of our systems. When the office retard traps us at the water cooler and begins to regale us with boring stories about his life, social custom tells us to listen for the shortest time possible and then make a polite escape. Unfortunately, in this situation we're left with some frustration or irritation at the minutes of our lives which have been irretrievably lost. In a perhaps ideal world, as soon as the bore started talking we would have grabbed the nearest heavy object and begun educating him with it in regards to wasting our time. This would have provided a release for us. However, the use of heavy objects in this way is generally frowned upon and so the frustration stays with us, at least for a time.

It's not only negative feelings which build up inside us. A parade of deliciously attractive members of an appealing gender at some event may leave your loins keen for some action while all you can do then and there is maybe clap quietly and say in a restrained voice, "How very nice!"

Any powerful emotional or sexual experience which we can't express due to either lack of opportunity or due to social constraints can also leave us emotionally or sexually charged and can linger inside us until we get a chance to get rid of it.

One process for cleaning out these emotions and nervous energy after the events which caused them is called catharsis. It's a purification or release of these emotions through intense or powerful experiences. Some people might use a run along the beach, heavy exercise at the gym, or some martial arts practice as a way of achieving this. However, working out this energy with your partner in the dungeon can be a better way to go because you can direct that built up tension and energy towards having a powerful scene with your partner. Putting that energy to use with your partner is going to do a whole lot more for your relationship than if you burn the energy solo, such as at a gym. To my mind this is a good way of doing things. Using BDSM scenes for catharsis provides benefits for both you and your partner rather than just for you alone.

Heavy handling, pain, being strung up by rope, humiliation play, and a whole range of other BDSM activities can be intense enough and powerful enough for catharsis. Just as with BDSM practised for recreation, cathartic BDSM can leave you feeling relieved and cleansed.

This catharsis is something BDSM folk may be achieving without actually thinking much about it. For some people—particular those who have had BDSM in their lives for a long time—scenes can be their best and most familiar way of discharging all this accumulated nervous energy and emotion. If they can't do scenes this energy will just keep building up. When this happens, the most obvious signs are that the person may become irritable or restless, sometimes without knowing why.

When someone doesn't recognise or realise that they use BDSM in this way, they may not give their BDSM scenes the attention which they should. As a result, BDSM scenes sometimes don't happen or aren't intense enough, the result being the irritability or restlessness which I mentioned above, or worse.

"Worse" can be when the people involved aren't consciously aware of the connection between their BDSM activities and the release of this pent-up energy. Instead of controlling it or finding other avenues to let it out—such as a visit to the gym—or by just simmering through it until it dissipates, they may start acting out. Without knowing why, they may start trying to goad their partner—perhaps behaving badly so that they get punished and, hence, get the pain or intense experience they were needing. This is not ideal and will put a strain on the relationship.

When a serious need for catharsis arises, the scenes which provide it need to be planned, time needs to be allocated, and whatever is required to make sure it comes off needs to be done. When they aren't given the priority they deserve, these BDSM scenes can easily fall off the planning wagon and not happen at all.

They can also fail to happen, or happen but not be satisfying, because:

- Your new partner doesn't like the same things your last partner did and so doesn't do the things which customarily lead to your catharsis,

- Your new partner prefers to do BDSM less frequently than you need,

- One of you is focussing on something else—such as kinky sex—and neglecting what needs to be done for their partner to feel cleansed,

- Medical reasons—broken bones, illness, etc., or

- Other things happening in other parts of your lives which leave you or your partner too tired or too distracted to scene.

Questions

1. Do you or your partner feel cleansed after some or all of your scenes?

2. How important is this experience of feeling cleansed? Is it a great relief? Do you feel like a weight has been taken from your shoulders? Do you feel more free after scenes?

3. What is it like when you can't scene or when you can't get this relief?

4. If scening isn't possible, how can you or your partner get catharsis?

6.21   Super-hot sex

While it's a topic that I'm cautious about discussing in terms of BDSM, sex just can't be avoided. The reason why I'm cautious talking about sex is because there are a lot of people who think that BDSM is only about sex. I'm concerned that if I talk about it too much it'll encourage them not to look any further than the bits between their legs. There's more to BDSM than sex, much more, and I'm hoping that through these books you're seeing just that.

That said, many people look at BDSM as a way of making sex more exciting and powerful than it would normally be in a vanilla context. This is an admirable goal and one which I fully support. There are a few ways this can work.

Firstly, even though we live in a liberated society, there are still some things which you generally don't talk about with your parents. BDSM is one of them. Because of this, BDSM acquires a sort of secretive or illicit feel to it. Mixing a hint of BDSM into your bedroom games might therefore add a little thrill from doing the forbidden. Even for those folk who limit themselves to fluffy handcuffs, or those who use silk handkerchiefs to tie their partner's arms and legs to the corners of the bed, this can be quite exciting. It can add an extra charge to sex. It may be that the buzz comes from fulfilling a secret fantasy, from actually or symbolically opening yourself up to your partner more than you might normally do, or it may come from doing something risque, something which you know that your parents or closest friends would disapprove of.

Secondly, sex is often an opportunity for you and your partner to intimately share each other's bodies and feelings. An important part is them being able to feel you, and you being able to feel them. Sex, of course, provides this in abundance.

Cocks and cunts have an enormous number of nerve endings all waiting to really make your day and sex makes them get up and dance. But in vanilla sex this is about all that happens. BDSM adds to how much you can penetrate your partner, to how much they can feel you, and to how much you can feel them. This is not necessarily about sticking things into your partner—though you could argue that the BDSM activities of cutting and piercing fit this description. Instead, I'm talking about our ability to use BDSM to create intense experiences and feelings with our partner beyond mere sex.

In vanilla sex for example, foreplay might consist of fondling, massage, soft music, dirty movies, an expensive dinner, or some combination of the above. These are nice, but they're not really that powerful.

Compare them to stringing your partner up to a bondage frame, tying them so tightly that they can't move, then teasing or torturing them with pincers or clamps on their sensitive bits, and exploring their genitals without them being able to move to stop you; or imagine starting out with a gentle caning and working up to an intense and heavy hammering of their butt; or imagine stripping your partner naked, pushing them around roughly, and wrestling them to the ground. Consider what it's like when you're on the receiving end of these things. There is power and intensity written all over these activities. Whether you're a dominant or a submissive involved in scenes like this, the scope for having a deep and penetrating awareness of your partner is much higher than, say, by sharing a dirty movie and some popcorn.

And then you add actual sexual intercourse on top of it.

Of course BDSM sex is hotter than vanilla sex!

How to enhance the experience

- Put aside your fears. Fear is one of the main things that gets in the way of fully immersing yourself in the experience you have with your partner. It creates barriers and limits how much they can penetrate you. That doesn't mean that you should be careless or take unnecessary risks. But once you and your partner have looked at the risks, made the right preparations, and taken the right precautions, then do allow yourself to be in the moment with your partner.

- Open yourself up. You can open yourself up physically by perhaps undressing and spreading your legs. However, there's much more to it in BDSM than that. BDSM can be a very intimate, shared journey, and when it is this makes sex much more powerful and intense. But for it to be intimate and shared you need to let your feelings, your desires, your hungers, and your lusts out where your partner can see them. When you feel something, don't hide it. Talk about your feelings and lusts. Demonstrate them. Show them. By doing so you create opportunities for your partner to go places with you, to explore you, and to see you as never before.

- Communicate more with your partner before, during, and even after sex. Use words, facial expressions, and gestures. Some people hold back from letting their partner know how they feel either during BDSM scenes or in the course of an ongoing BDSM relationship. In a scene they may be too caught up in ecstasy to speak, or they may not want to distract their partner when their partner seems to be having such a good time. But by holding back you prevent your partner from experiencing you. They don't know and can't feel you unless they get some sort of message such as an occasional grunt, wriggle, or groan; or even the occasional, "That is soooo HOT!"

- Likewise, encourage your partner to let loose with grunts, groans, and expressions of amazement at the feelings you're giving them. This will help you to feel them more.

Vanilla sex can be limiting as its focus is often mere genital-on-genital friction. Adding in BDSM, actively exploring dominance or submission before or during the act, or adding in intense physical feelings through bondage, torture or impact play, can double or triple the feelings, closeness, and responsiveness. Rather than just limiting the action to the area between the hips and thighs, BDSM lets psychological play and other forms of engagement take place at the same time.

I've noted that much of BDSM in the context of a relationship is about penetration, about you and your partner deeply and deliberately experiencing and feeling each other. By combining BDSM and sex we get penetration occurring not just sexually—i.e., cock-in-cunt—but psychologically, emotionally, and maybe even elsewhere physically on your bodies. This means that instead of the focus mainly being your dick or your cunt, your whole body and mind, and those of your partner can be and are fully involved.

Questions

- For you, what is the next step up from vanilla sex?

- Which aspects of combining BDSM activities with sex do you find hot?

- If you're already an experienced BDSMer, do you ever engage in sex with a vanilla partner? How is it different to BDSM sex?

- Do you find it difficult to let yourself go? Why?

Chapter 7

Dominance and submission

The most visible style of BDSM has to do with physical pain, physical sensation, and physical restraint. It involves activities such as cutting, bondage, cages, gags, hoods, caning, whipping, wax play, spanking, and so on. For many folk, these physical activities are the tools they use to achieve their own particular outcomes. Causing intense pain might lead to catharsis, tight rope bondage might lead to a physiological release, sensual flogging might lead to heightened sexual arousal and then to hotter sex with partners, etc., etc.

There are other people for whom the exercise of power or the experience of power are the tools. Instead of using physical sensation, we could say that they use psychological or emotional sensation. For them the exploration and the exercise of power, authority, and control are the most interesting, powerful, satisfying, and rewarding parts of their BDSM. What they do to and with each other physically is less important than the opportunities which their activities give them to express and experience power. The physical results of these explorations—such as the red butt, the bruises, or the tangle of rope and knots—may simply be icing on an already satisfying and delicious cake.

It can sometimes be difficult to separate the physical side of BDSM and the psychological. I might order my submissive or slave to her knees and firmly push her head down as she does so. The main part of this for us both might be the effect of the exercise of my authority, but pushing her head down adds a physical aspect which reinforces the psychological. If I just told her to kneel and pushed her head down without having underlying power or authority the effect and the outcome for us both would be very different and certainly far less satisfying.

The deliberate exploration of power, authority, and control is the realm of dominance and submission (D&s) and mastery and slavery (M/s). While this might not be discussed much in vanilla or conservative company, as I've noted earlier[1], research shows that exploring and experiencing power motivates many people's intimate relationships with as many as 20% or more of men and women saying that this is significant for them. Even so, because of the common focus on the physical side of BDSM, many people don't realise the extent to which power and authority are being actively utilised in their relationships because it is obscured by the physical activities which go along with them. This may be because they simply don't notice or

---

[1] Section 6.8 on page 45.

are too busy with the physical aspects of their play, or it can also be because accepting that they enjoy taking control of their partner or that they enjoy being controlled by their partner may be uncomfortable thoughts.

Understanding the role of power and authority can help you with your relationship. If authoritatively pressing your submissive to their knees, or if being pressed to your knees by your dominant is effective for you beyond the mere physical force which is used, then there may be a significant D&s component involved. Recognising that this is so lets you focus on and use this in addition to any physical BDSM you practice, potentially multiplying the satisfaction and penetration for you and your partner.

Power is like the electricity you get out of a wall socket. You might have a reassuring feeling that it'll be there when you need it, but it's not actually providing you with any benefit until you plug something in and start using it. Likewise, just having power in a BDSM relationship is not enough. Actually using power over your partner or feeling your partner using their power over you is what makes D&s or M/s effective for both of you. The physical aspect might still be rewarding, but taking away the exercise of power and just leaving the mechanical or physical side of BDSM may not be enough.

Power comes in many different forms. Physical strength, intellectual superiority, and diabolical cleverness are three examples. But something like the ability and readiness to inflict pain can also be power. It is something which can be used to control your partner. It is also something which many people don't have. That's not to say that it's sadism *per se*, but actually using pain or inflicting pain are not things which are very common or supported in our society, and being comfortably able to do so is another tool in your BDSM toolbox.

Anyway, there are many forms of power which are relevant to BDSM. Below is a list of activities or scenarios in which different forms of power or authority can be exercised. When you're reading through these, try and separate out in your own mind the difference between the power itself and the activities which make the power felt. Note that in many cases the activities involved aren't the flogging, caning, or bondage which are typically associated with BDSM.

7.1 Different types or forms of D&s

- Physical domination - Many people respond positively to being physically manipulated or manhandled, dragged by the hair, choked, pushed to the ground, and so on. This sort of domination can include erotic wrestling and even lightweight activities such as taking your partner's arm and guiding them to where you want them to go.

  It isn't always necessary for the dominant to be physically stronger than their submissive. In many cases, the fact that the dominant attempts to use strength or force is enough for the submissive to surrender.

- Domination through pain - This is the use of pain to manipulate feelings and behaviour, or to cause reactions. Pain is a powerful tool in a dominant's toolbox because it is difficult to resist. It can be sharp or thuddy pain, such as from some types of floggers. Dried peas in shoes can be quite effective, as can grains of uncooked rice under the knees while kneeling. Many submissives will not be able to stop themselves responding to the pain or discomfort.

On the other hand, for some submissives the act of resisting is what they need. The pain they receive from their dominant is what they can struggle against in a similar way to how some bondage enthusiasts will struggle against their ropes once they are tied.

- Intellectual domination - This is dominating or over-whelming your submissive by knowing more, by having more experience, by being able to think more quickly, or by simply having a higher I.Q. than they do. For some submissives this gives them a reassuring feeling of being put in their place, while for others the use of intellect to dominate them gives them a way of challenging their dominant by struggling to compete against it.

- Emotional domination - Manipulating emotions, such as by creating and using fear, can also be an effective way for a submissive to feel the power or skills of their dominant.

- Humiliation - Manipulating the feelings of self-worth of a submissive—such as by insulting them, revealing their weaknesses, criticising their abilities, or by exposing embarrassing past or present behaviour—is another way in which a dominant can bring their submissive to feel both helplessness and an inability to resist.

- Objectification - Reducing someone to less than a person—such as by making them serve as a table or chair, or by treating them as merely a life-support system for their genitals, i.e., as a collection of bodily organs which keeps their cock or cunt alive—decreases their ability to value themselves and compels them instead to feel valued as much or as little as their dominant chooses. Again, this is an exercise in control and power. The dominant decides when, where, and how often to use this object, and decides the value of the object, i.e., the submissive.

- Military interrogation - This is a form of role play where the submissive or slave is typically tied or handcuffed to a chair. The dominant or master then uses pain, fear, or torture to get them to reveal certain secrets. In reality the dominant already knows the secrets, and the submissive knows this. The exercise is for the submissive to resist the dominant, and for the dominant to attempt to use whatever means necessary to get the submissive to yield. Note that sometimes the desired outcome is that the submissive successfully resists, rather than is broken.

- Manipulation of sensations - A dominant can take control of what sensations a submissive can experience by means of blindfolds, earplugs, or by wrapping them in soft material so they can't feel either with their fingers or with the rest of their skin.

- Manipulating situational awareness - Going further, blindfolds and earplugs can limit your submissive's ability to determine what is going on around them. You can cause your submissive to think something dangerous, confronting, or shocking is happening to them through misleading them, misinforming them, and through manipulating what they see, hear, or feel. This can be called a mind-fuck.

- Service-oriented domination (personal) - This is directing and controlling how your submissive performs different types of personal service. We can define personal service as something which has to do with a dominant's intimate or immediate wants and needs. These can include preparing or providing food, drink, or sex; acting as a personal assistant; providing entertainment in the form of singing, playing an instrument, or dancing; and so on. The important thing is that they directly involve the dominant. These sorts of interaction allow the submissive or slave to get instant feedback on their performance, and allows the dominant to retain fine control of their partner, or even to micromanage them.

- Service-oriented domination (impersonal) - Some submissives and slaves also respond to serving their dominant or master at a distance. This sort of impersonal service is where the actual service is performed away from the dominant, such as by doing household shopping or running other errands, attending training, performing household maintenance, editing master's literary creations, cleaning the car, and so on. The dominant initiates the service but then the submissive completes it on their own.

When we compare the personal and impersonal variations of this type of domination we can see that there are some parallels between these and physical BDSM activities which involve, on the one hand, a lot of physical interaction between the submissive and dominant (personal) and, on the other hand, those where the submissive is left to "soak", such as with mummification or longer-term static bondage (impersonal).

- Scene-only domination - The above two types of domination involve the submissive or slave performing useful service for their partner. The outcome is that something has been achieved—such as the shopping done, time saved for the dominant, or some pleasure has been given—such as sex or a yummy dinner. For some couples, simply spending time together with the dominant exercising his submissive by ordering her around—such as directing her to sit, stand, adopt particular postures, leading her using a leash, and so on—is satisfying on its own. In this case, the exercise of power is immediate and only lasts as long as the exercise period or scene.

- Role play-based domination - Scene-only domination can be combined with role play to create a context or style for the domination and submission. When the submissive adopts the role of a puppy for example, this allows the dominant to use their control and authority to train the submissive in that context. In this example, it could include toilet training, learning to sit, fetch, and so on. Mischievous behaviour can be tamed, discipline can be applied, and correct behaviour as defined by the dominant can be taught in this style of domination. Age play or infant play can also be used in this way.

- Hunter / prey domination - One aspect of D&s which is not often discussed is where the submissive actively attempts to evade or resist their dominant partner. This typically involves a form of challenge from the submissive and can be combined with one or more of the above types of domination.

  It can involve the dominant physically or symbolically pursuing, capturing, and possibly defeating the submissive. The use of diabolical cleverness is common from both the dominant and the submissive.

  For example, in straightforward military interrogation the interrogator (the dominant) might just impose gradually increasing levels of pain or suffering on their submissive partner. In response, the submissive might try to mislead or distract their dominant, try to exhaust them, or lead them to believe that they, the submissive, are close to breaking when they aren't. They might also try to deflect any pain—such as by turning or twisting during caning—or may try to escape the ropes when their dominant is looking away. Instead of the submissive being a willing and receptive target for the dominant, the submissive resists and effectively challenges their dominant to defeat them. It can become a hard game of D&s-flavoured cat-and-mouse.

Physical domination can often be symbolic. A small woman may be able to physically dominate a much bigger and stronger man simply by pushing or exerting nominal strength. For both, it may be the symbolism which is important. However, physical domination can become a genuine battle which the submissive may not always be guaranteed to lose and where the dominant needs to actually overwhelm their resisting partner, pin them down, and force them to yield.

Predicament bondage is a challenge-based style of bondage where the top or dominant ties their partner in an uncomfortable position but leaves some leeway to allow their partner to find a better or more comfortable position. Often though, the options available to the submissive are designed by their partner to only allow an exchange of one sort of discomfort for another. Should the submissive manage to temporarily find some bodily contortion which gives them some unexpected comfort—and thus defeat their dominant—their dominant ups the challenge by adding another rope or knot to remove the solution the submissive found.

It is not uncommon for a submissive to challenge their dominant anyway, just in the normal course of things. Submissives who like or need to be dominated by their partner often look for reassurance that their dominant is still up to the task. Rather than going through the motions, sometimes they try to challenge or resist in small or large ways to experience their partner's reaction, which could be to correct their submissive, discipline them, or whatever.

All of the above provide opportunities for domination and submission to occur. They create a context in which the outcome—the feelings and experiences of the people involved—is heavily influenced by the power and the authority the dominant uses, and by how the submissive responds to these. This is different to scenes and activities which are primarily physical, such as flogging or cutting, where the actual execution of the physical activity is far more important than the power or authority behind the execution.

Not all of the different types of domination I listed above will be effective for everybody. Which ones work and which ones don't will depend on your needs at the time, on your past experiences, and on other factors. It's worth sitting down with your partner and asking yourselves:

- Which of the activities are attractive to you?

- Do any of them scare you?

- Are there times or moods in which some activities would be more appealing or satisfying to you than others?

Dominance and submission

- Would the range of activities be different when you're horny? Whey you're tired? When you're just home from a stressful day at the office? At the beginning of a long weekend? Any time?

- Which of these activities work for your partner? When?

- Which of your partner's needs can they satisfy?

- What is the role of physical domination for you? Is physically overwhelming or overpowering your partner satisfying for you and them?

- What is the role of intellectual domination for you? Is being outwitted or out-thought important?

- Is the role of pain important to your explorations of dominance and submission?

- Do you want to maintain the feeling of dominance over your partner outside of the dungeon or away from where you play?

- Do you want to be constantly aware of your partner's dominance over you?

- Do you want to limit the dominance and submission to strict times when you play together?

While you're considering all of the above, another important question is:

- Which of the above types of domination or ways of using power definitely won't work for you or your partner? Which of them would be counterproductive to the goals and motivations you and your partner have for your BDSM?

Some expressions of power and control can cause bad or negative feelings. For example, physical domination for some rape victims, intellectual domination for people who lack self-confidence, or manipulating sensations combined with a blindfold for someone afraid of the dark. You need to discuss with your partner the ways of using power which push your buttons, the ways which cause problems for you, and the ways which are simply uninteresting.

From the list above we may notice that some D&s can be conflict-based. The dominant has power and the submissive resists or fights against it. Hunter/prey is a case in point, as can be intellectual domination, military interrogation, and even some forms of predicament bondage. Where conflict or resistance is a key factor, where resisting and then being overwhelmed is a possibility, you need to recognise that the idea of defeat has now entered the picture. For some submissives, giving their dominant a good run for their money is important and empowering, while for others the need to be actually and fully defeated is a vital component. Likewise, many dominants like or need the thrill of the chase and don't necessarily want an easy victory. Indeed, some just want the chase and aren't interested in victory. Knowing when and if you should actually defeat your partner, or be defeated by them, is something you should discuss with them.

When there is this element of conflict or resistance to your D&s, a good way to ensure that your submissive is not defeated, and that they don't appear to have gotten the better of you (which is a bad look), is to constrain your activities to a time limit. When your military interrogation, for example, reaches the time limit, you stop and congratulate your partner on being one tough cookie and not having given in. They then applaud your clever ways of torturing them.

Dominance and submission

All of the things I listed earlier are ways of making power and control felt. This can either be the feeling of being controlled by your partner, or the feeling of power over your partner. In an earlier book of mine, *The Control Book*[2], I looked at the mechanics of control in a BDSM-style relationship, at the taking of control, at the use of control, at reinforcing control, at releasing control, and so on. If you want more detail, please look there.

It's important to note that controlling your partner or being controlled by your partner need not have anything to do with the standard array of BDSM implements—such as floggers, whips, leather catsuits, needles, hooks, and so on. Indeed, some people can have control-based relationships with their partner and there's hardly a BDSM implement in sight. It can simply be enough for one partner to be willing to take charge and the other to follow.

This sort of subtle power difference between two people can manifest itself in the bedroom by who prefers to be on top and who prefers to be on the bottom. Other times it can be hinted at by who predominately chooses restaurants, who walks in front, and who asks whom which clothes look best (i.e., seeking approval from their partner).

If you do want or need control to be an important part of the relationship you have with your partner, there are some things you need to do.

---

[2][MASTERS2009]

7.2 Determine why

For dominants

You need to have a clear idea of which of your wants and needs are going to be met by dominating or mastering your partner. These can anything from the prosaic to the rare and unusual:

- You might find that grabbing your partner by the scruff of the neck, tearing off their clothes, and then having your wicked way with them turns you on sexually. Sometimes surprisingly, this can also be exciting and satisfying for a variety of partners.

- You may find it cathartic at the end of the day to simply bend your naked partner over a table, flog them to release your tensions, and then fuck them.

- You might find that it feels exciting and empowering to have your partner trained up so that they act almost as an extension of yourself, being tuned in to your priorities and values, and able to participate in and contribute to your projects almost as if you were doing them yourself.

- You may find it powerful and exciting to see your highly-talented, smart, and attractive partner surrendering themselves willingly to your directions as you make choices for them, give them orders, and set tasks for them.

- You might also find it intense and stimulating to use your personal authority and power to compel your partner's helpless obedience in anything from trivial exercises in micromanagement to complex choreographed scenes of behaviour.

- Dominating your partner might create opportunities for fun and playfulness, such as teasing, tickling, or taunting your partner.

Some submissives and slaves really do blossom when they have a strong and effective dominant or master in their lives. Be cautious about this being a one-way thing. You may get an initial rush out of seeing your partner respond to you, and you may feel motivated to put in a lot of effort to achieve this, but if all you really get out of it is that you see them blossom and then they pack up and leave, then you've received the short end of the stick.

This is all about having a good relationship, not being sucked dry. On the other hand, if having your partner blossom enriches both your lives and creates new and exciting possibilities, go for it.

For submissives

As a submissive, you also need to have a clear idea of why you want to be dominated by your partner. Some submissives seem to have the idea that being dominated means endless orgasms, and that the good times roll on without them having to do very much at all except make their genitals available. If you can find someone who calls themselves a dominant and who is happy to go along with this, then by all means proceed full steam ahead.

Otherwise, if you want or need control over you by your partner to be a part of your relationship, then you need to work out why. What's in it for you? At this point don't worry about what your partner gets out of it because this is something they need to work out for themselves.

- Are you looking for hotter sex?

- Do you enjoy the feeling of being physically handled by your partner?

- Do you find it empowering to surrender to their personal needs? In other words, is providing personal or intimate service to them—such as serving them food or drinks, attending to their needs at home, or serving them sexually—a strong motivator for you?

- How strongly or strictly do you want them to control you? Do you want them to be strict with you? Lenient? Tolerant? Playful? Turn a blind eye?

- Do you respond strongly to being a servant or by doing menial or simple labour for them such as cleaning duties, gardening, errands, etc.?

- Or do you want to be a co-worker in their lives, contributing to their projects or community causes?

- Are you looking for a partner who will create a framework of rules and standards in which they expect you to operate? In other words, do you want or need your partner to set standards of behaviour and boundaries for you? Do you want them to shape how you behave, how you speak, etc.?

7.3 Determine the scope of the control

For dominants

It can be easy to say that you want complete control, but do you really want to be involved in deciding what size underwear they buy? Or which way they drive to the supermarket? Or which particular salad they have for lunch? Or how many of those little plastic soy sauce fish thingies they use on their sushi?

You need to realistically look at what will be useful and productive for you to control and what will be a burden.

- Are you just interested in a bit of heavy-handling of your submissive one or two evenings per week, perhaps with some oral sex (performed by them, of course), and the rest of the time they make up their own mind about things?

- Do you look forward to sitting them down at your feet each evening, discussing their day with them, and giving them directions for the next day(s)?

- Do you like choosing your partner's clothes for when they go out?

- Do you enjoy having them serve you meals when you're at home?

- Do you enjoy having them serve you in other ways at home—doing the housework, doing the cooking, doing the cleaning, doing the shopping?

- Do you want to keep them naked and available for you sexually when you're both at home?

- Do you want to involve your partner in your projects and have them work alongside you?

This is one of the big parts of being a dominant. You need to have a clear idea of what you want. Your submissive partner is going to respond to your decisiveness and determination. This comes from the strength of your feelings and needs. Merely wanting them to do something, like lick or suck your genitals 24 hours per day, is not enough. You have to have the determination and drive to take control and compel their obedience. Otherwise it's not really dominance, and it can descend into mere asking or even begging.

So, make a distinction between what you just would like, and what you are prepared to pursue and take.

For submissives

Saying that you want your dominant to have complete control may sound good and feel right when you are in the throes of passion in the dungeon, but in real life there are frequently areas where your partner should absolutely not have any influence. At the same time, for D&s to work for you there probably need to be things that definitely do need to be controlled.

- What's off-limits?

    - Finances?
    - Your job, such as being required by your dominant to wear clothes to work which are inappropriate?
    - Your family, children, and other dependents?
    - Your pets?
    - Your insurance policies and retirement planning?
    - The house or property you own?
    - Your car?
    - Your health and medical treatment?

Dominance and submission

- What do you definitely want them to control?

  - Your pink bits?
  - All the activities which aren't determined to be off-limits?
  - What and when you eat?
  - Who you socialise with?
  - When and how you speak?
  - Your use of alcohol?
  - Your choice of clothes, perfume, and deodorant?

- When do the above apply?

  - Is this just in the dungeon?
  - Just on dungeon nights?
  - Just when you've discussed it and agreed to it?
  - Just outside the dungeon?
  - All the time?

7.4 Determine how

For a dominant, having someone available 24/7 to whom all manner of nefarious things can be done, or who may be called upon to bend over backwards to serve you in various ways, is a tantalising and often powerful thought. Similarly, for a submissive, the idea of having a master or dominant who is always ready with a rope or an authoritative word can create deep and powerful sexual or emotional stirrings.

How do you make this happen though?

For dominants

Dominants and masters need to have an idea about what they're after from their partner. There are many dominants and masters whose goals seem to consist exclusively of getting their partner horny and "giving" them orgasms, perhaps as a leg-opener. This may seem to be the reverse of the way things ought to be done, i.e., with the submissive or slave serving their partner rather than the other way around.

Dominance is about establishing, maintaining, and using authority and power over your partner. Once you have established this authority then the quick fuck, or the cooked dinner, or the help with a personal project become a natural part of that framework.

Authority and power become manifest, they become felt and tangible, when there is a goal or when there is an intensity of purpose behind them. If you have no goal then neither of you will feel anything. If your submissive has agreed to anything you want and the best you can come up with is, "I order you to do what you want!", or "With all the authority vested in me I don't particularly command you to do anything much at all!", then you might just as well not have the power or authority at all.

What you need to do is read through the list of types of D&s earlier in this chapter[3] and see whether any of these seem powerful to you. I deliberately used the word "powerful" here because power is generally what you need to feel for D&s to work. If you instead find the things in the list only arousing, intense, exciting, profound, cleansing, or anything else, then

---

[3] Section 7.1 on page 86.

Dominance and submission

perhaps D&s isn't what you should be working on. But, if the adjective "powerful" applies to what you feel then maybe D&s is where you should be focusing more or all of your energy.

For submissives

As a submissive you also need to work out how D&s will work for you. The same list of different types of D&s earlier in this chapter may be a help to you in at least crossing out the things which you are sure aren't going to be suitable for you, and may help you find some things which you're sure will be.

Reflect on things you have experienced—both in BDSM and in vanilla experiences—which seemed to trigger something inside you. Do you find that visits to the doctor where you have to undress or be probed are "interesting"? Is being directed by a burly man in a policeman's uniform a turn on? Is being tortured by your partner powerful just because they like seeing you in that situation? Is being treated as a table or footstool rewarding? In sum, how important is power to you?

7.5   Purpose and conviction

For dominants

I can't stress this enough: when you're the dominant or master in a 24/7 relationship then the things which are going to give you the most mileage are purpose and conviction.

If you think that owning a slave or having a submissive is a really great idea... well, maybe it is. But if this idea comes first, or if all you have is the idea and that's what turns you on then you've probably put the cart before the horse. Acquiring a slave or submissive and then working out what to do with them is not the way to go.

Instead, you need to have a goal, a purpose, or an intention which requires two people, and then you find a submissive or slave who can be a part of making that goal into reality.

Many dominants and masters fall into the trap of looking for a submissive or slave with the hope that they'll then get inspired, or that the needs and wants of their new submissive partner will set them and the new relationship off in some useful direction. Perhaps we should call this submissive-driven dominance because the submissive is the one who ends up determining what happens. For a submissive who likes to top from the bottom, this might be a good thing.

However, there are many submissives and slaves who are going to respond to the strength of purpose of their dominant or master. Indeed, they may need this. Instead of being the ones who are doing the driving, these are the ones who need to be driven, who need to submit or surrender to the strength and power of their partner. In D&s, this strength often comes from the purpose or goals of the dominant.

When you have a dominant who looks for inspiration from his submissive partner, or a master who directs his slave based on his slave's wants, then you can end up in serious conflict when they're matched up against a slave or submissive who needs to surrender to their dominant or master. Neither partner will get anywhere because each will be waiting for inspiration or direction from the other.

There are many different sorts of uses to which you can put your submissive or slave, but the key things are that there's some passion or drive of yours involved, and that they get to feel that you are putting them to good use. Many submissives are delighted to be useful, and while you shouldn't try to just create work for them, recognising opportunities where they can do the things you might ordinarily do yourself can be quite effective for you both.

For example:

- You direct your submissive to assist you in preparing or cleaning the dungeon for the night's activities.

- Send them out to buy you something you need when you are busy with something else.

- Put them in charge of some aspect of running the household such as making the bed, or preparing breakfast each day. You set the standard of work and supervise them, or check up on them at intervals (e.g., weekly).

- Have them assist you in running some personal project such as a web log, BDSM dating website, or newsletter. You should be chief editor, and they would be your assistant editor, researcher, or whatever.

- Have them be your driver when you go places together.

- Of course, sex is a common theme in many people's BDSM and there's no reason why sex can't be a purpose or goal, such as daily oral sex.

- If you really like tying them up, then require your partner to be your bondage bunny.

When you are planning on having a D&s or M/s relationship, before you even start looking for someone to have it with, you need to work out what you are wanting to achieve with them and the relationship. Especially in D&s and M/s relationships, your partner will be needing you to know where the relationship is going, and to have some idea of how to get there. If you don't know these things then it means that either the relationship is going to be a dud or that your submissive/slave partner is going to have to take over to some extent and provide direction... and this is probably a poor outcome for you both.

So, determine your goals, how strongly you feel about them, how long it'll take to achieve them (if they are goals with an end), and the sort of slave or submissive you'll need to get there.

Once you know these things, you need to ask yourself whether what you're looking for is something that is part-time or full-time. If it is strictly related to needs-meeting then maybe a part-time or casual relationship will work. If it's something ongoing or that needs more frequent interactions then maybe a full-time, live-in relationship is in order.

In any case, once you know these things—and not before—you're ready to find a submissive or slave to be your partner in this. They also need to know up front what the goals are and how you're going to achieve them because they need to know whether all this is going to satisfy their own BDSM wants and needs.

For submissives

While it might seem that purpose and conviction are character-istics of a dominant, a submissive or slave also needs that sense of purpose. If you're hoping that your dominant is going to take charge and make everything wonderful then think again. You too have an important and active part in this.

Dominance and submission

Your purpose is to surrender to your partner. You need to be physically, psychologically, and emotionally available for this to happen. If your partner grabs you by the scruff of the neck and you don't surrender then they may still get their way, but it may not be that rewarding for you. Whenever you dig your heels in and reject their use of their power—maybe because you feel rotten, have had a fight or a hard day at work, or because you have a headache—then the good times will certainly not roll. Digging your heels in is your choice. I'm not saying here that you should necessarily force yourself to be available, but you do need to recognise that a big part of being a submissive or slave is being ready, willing, and able, even when the time is not right for you. To dominate you, your partner needs to choose the time that is right for them. If they always choose times which are right for you then they're not dominating you or compelling you at all.

Self-focussed and other-focussed

Another way of considering this is by determining where your focus lies when you're engaging your partner. If you're focussed on the feelings and experience you are having, then you're self-focussed. If you are instead focussing all of your attention on the feelings and reactions of your partner then you are other-focussed.

If you're a dominant or top flogging your partner and the action is making you so horny that you can barely keep your hands off your partner then you're self-focussed. If instead you're paying very close attention to the twitches and moans of your partner as you work them up into a lather of rhapsodic ecstasy then you're focussing on them—you're other-focussed.

From the other side, if when you bring your partner a drink it gives you butterflies or makes you feel all gooey inside then you're self-focussed. If you're paying keen attention to what your partner is doing so that you can anticipate their needs before they even realise them themselves, then you're other-focussed.

There's nothing right or wrong about being self-focussed or other-focussed. Both are powerful and potentially very satisfying and productive for your relationship. One is neither better nor worse than the other. It is important though, that when you're being self-focussed that your partner is being other-focussed or vice versa. Self- and other-focus are complementary. Two people who are only other-focussed are not going to have a lot of joy, and nor are two people who are only self-focussed.

Focus changes frequently. A dominant might easily be self-focussed most of the time during a scene, but switch his focus to his partner from time to time and at the end of the scene to make sure she is OK while still staying dominant the whole time. A submissive also might switch her focus back and forth between herself and her partner as they interact. It is often the case that a particular person will be primarily one or the other—i.e., self-focussed or other-focussed—in their preferred style of play or engagement.

Dominance and submission

7.6 Service

Earlier in this chapter, where I listed different types of D&s[4], I mentioned personal and impersonal service. Service in BDSM can be a complex thing to appreciate. In any relationship between two people, wants and needs must be addressed on both sides for the relationship to meet its goals of contributing to the satisfaction or pleasure of the two people involved. This is a type of exchange where each person both contributes something to the relationship and also takes something out of the relationship. The end result is that both are happier, more satisfied, more complete, or more content than they would be flying solo.

In this sense, both people—be they dominant, submissive, master, or slave—serve. They both make an effort to satisfy the needs of the relationship and consequently their partner.

Any personal or impersonal service in this context is very different to what you might find in a professional service relationship such as with a butler, housemaid, cook, or valet. Firstly, and obviously, there is no salary for a BDSM submissive or slave; they're not there for the money or the job. Secondly, although what they do and how they're treated may have some superficial resemblance at times to a butler or housemaid, the wants and needs behind this service do not. Because we're talking about BDSM, the motivations behind service—either serving or being served—include just about all the motivations I listed in the previous chapter. Minimising self, recreation, hotter sex, catharsis, and so on are all possible through service. Indeed, the sort of profound surrender to service which is sometimes

---

[4] Section 7.1 on page 86.

found in BDSM can be an amazing, beautiful, and humbling thing.

If service is of interest to you, to get the most out of serving or being served, you should know the answers to these basic questions:

- What do you want to get out of service?

- What are you giving in return?

The above questions, by the way, apply equally to dominants, submissives, masters and slaves. Don't expect your own answers to these questions to be either short or simple. BDSM is often about multiple wants and needs rather than just one, and so what you or your partner are looking for may involve any number of motivations, and these motivations may vary depending on circumstances.

For example, consider a master and a slave. What service wants or needs might be involved for the slave? The answer may be a combination of things:

- The master may use the slave as an outlet for the master's own sadistic drives, or as a part of their own catharsis. As they whale into their slave with a heavy flogger or whip they are, at the same time, releasing nervous energy or stress which might have built up inside them. The slave might be using this same flogging in their own way:

  - As a means to achieve their own catharsis,

  - As a way of experiencing deep surrender to the wants or needs of their partner by suffering the pain their master needs to give them, or

Dominance and submission

- As a way of demonstrating their devotion to their partner/master by their stoic endurance of whatever their master can quite literally throw at them.

- The slave may use service partly as an expression of their devotion to someone they admire and respect, ie., their master. It's important to note that the master earns this devotion both by their previous behaviour—such as by being a respected teacher in the local community, a ready support for others in need, etc.—and by how they behave towards the slave ongoing.

- A significant aspect of being a slave is that of supporting or creating situations in which a master can be a master. For example, an important part of BDSM is the disparity of power. By being more assertive, more authoritative, more passionate, or more intense, the master can express this power difference and help the slave surrender to it. At the same time though, the slave is serving the master by being the tool they use to express this power difference.

  If the slave has wants or needs which are best met through some particular BDSM activity—such as cutting, bondage, whipping, etc.—then the master can exploit his skills in these areas so that the slave feels that he is at the master's mercy in regards to having these needs met. Again, in this situation the slave is also serving as a tool which the master uses to feel "masterly".

  If the master is far more experienced than the slave in matters relating to BDSM, the master can continuously challenge the slave in areas to do with service, obedience, and surrender. Again, this allows the slave to feel the power and superior skills of the master and allows the master to express himself as a master.

And if the master is more knowledgeable, or even more intelligent than the slave, the master can use this to compel the slave's surrender to the master's greater knowledge and understanding. It's important here to note that this isn't about diminishing or humiliating the slave and making them feel less important or less valuable. It is instead about the master using his skills to explore power over the submissive. Remember that this is also rewarding for the master who should [hopefully] see the slave as a valuable partner and critical component in this mutually-satisfying exercise in power.

7.7 Service dominants

While it's common to think of service being provided by a slave or by a submissive, we can also have *service dominants*. They often make their appearance in scenes involving the submissive or slave having orgasms. This is something I occasionally find weird because the dominants involved seem to think they are in charge when they're actually being completely guided by their slave's or submissive's own sexual responsiveness.

If you find it exciting that you can play orgasm-denial games with your partner to such an extent that when they finally come they can be heard across half the country, isn't it really your slave's or submissive's sexual abilities which are controlling you? If they needed their clitoris wiggled in one particular way to get them more horny then aren't you compelled to obey the clitoris? There's nothing wrong with actually doing these sorts of shenanigans and, in fact, they can be enormous fun, but I like to call a spade a spade and say where the control really lays. This is because one of my themes here is engagement, and you get the best engagement when you're recognising the reality of what's going on. The point is that what you do with your partner, and what they do with you is rewarding, fully engaging, and satisfying to you both.

No matter how dominant or authoritative a dominant or master is, if the goal is to bring his slave or submissive to orgasm, or to have her cry out in agony from a heavy whipping, or to send him into blissful sub-space, then the master or dominant must provide what the submissive needs so they react that way, i.e., so they come, yell, or whatever.

The dominant or master may be the one who decides that service is to occur, but when it is the slave's or submissive's needs being met, it is the slave or submissive who determines what has to be done.

7.8   Discussion

Dominance and submission come in a variety of flavours—such as physical domination, mind fucks, and so on—and some people will have their own preferences. But just as some days I prefer lemon gelato, there are other days when I like strawberry or vanilla or chocolate. The various flavours of dominance and submission each satisfy particular hungers and desires. There is no need to identify yourself with one particular style or flavour of D&s. More you should consider how well each one works for you and your partner in different circumstances.

Even when one particular style of D&s works for you and your partner most of the time, changes to your own circumstances, changes to why you are doing D&s, and even jadedness from over-familiarity can mean that it's time for you to try something new. The lists and discussions in this chapter should give you some ideas.

7.9 Questions

- How do you differentiate between artful domination and psychological abuse[5]?

- What can you do casually with someone (e.g., someone you meet at a party) which can be exciting, rewarding, or satisfying in a D&s sense? Something service-related? Training? Physical handling? Sex? Something else?

- Things to do or not do:

  - What things should a dominant do in a D&s relationship?

  - What things should a dominant NOT do in a D&s relationship?

  - What things should a submissive do in a D&s relationship?

  - What things should a submissive NOT do in a D&s relationship?

- Does fear have a role to play in D&s relationships? If so, fear of what? How does it contribute?

---

[5]While I'm just posing this as a question here for you to think about, if you're interested in more of my words on the topic I did devote a whole chapter to abuse in another of my books, *This Curious Human Phenomenon* [MASTERS2008, ch. 21, pp. 209 - 223].

- Can fear be an indicator of an abusive D&s relationship? For the dominant? For the submissive?

- Activities:

  - Which activities, behaviours, and attitudes (either in you or your partner) have helped develop and reinforce the experience of D&s for you? Where does the feeling of power come from?

  - Which activities, behaviours, and attitudes have worked against or diminished the experience of D&s for you?

  - Are there any styles or flavours of D&s which definitely don't work for you or your partner? Why?

  - Are there any styles or flavours of D&s which only work at certain times for you and your partner such as:

    * When you don't have much time?
    * When you're on holidays and completely relaxed?
    * When the day has been busy or stressful and you're unwinding?

Chapter 8

The lists

One of the challenges of BDSM can be finding ways to express each of your BDSM feelings, desires, and needs when you're with your partner. While rope bondage and flogging are common, just because they work for some people doesn't mean that they're going to work for you, or that there won't be times when they're not enough and you're needing something else.

In this chapter I have listed some 200+ BDSM activities and sorted them into different categories. These lists can help you in a couple of ways:

- Firstly, they can serve as inspiration and a source of ideas. As you read through these lists with your partner, you may find activities which neither of you have thought of exploring before.

  There may be activities which you prefer, but doing the same thing all the time can sometimes become a bit stale, even when it is exciting, satisfying, and fun most of the time. Having a rich BDSM repertoire can help you make sure that you're ready for the times when you and your partner want something new, something different, something particularly intense, or just a little fun.

- Secondly, as you read through these lists you may start to see patterns in the sorts of things which appeal to you. This might help you understand what you want out of BDSM, different ways in which you might be able to get it, and what this means for the sort of BDSM partner and relationship you need.

  For example, you may discover that impact play is a common factor in all of the activities which push your buttons, or you might find that you like your BDSM to be strictly limited to scenes involving chains, or you might find that anything involving having your partner helpless at your feet is what rocks your boat. Knowing these things helps you target what you do so that you get the most out of it.

Keep in mind that this book is about relationships rather than being a how-to guide of super kinky things to do with your partner. For this reason I haven't attempted to explain how to do any of the activities I list here, but if you are keen to find out more about them, or to try them and don't know how, then have a look at the practical guides on my own web site[1], or check out your local kinky bookstore or Amazon.com[2].

---

[1] http://www.peter-masters.com/
[2] http://www.amazon.com/

Revisiting the lists in this chapter from time to time can also be useful. As you get more experience in BDSM, and as your own skills and abilities develop, some activities which were once uninteresting, unappealing, or even impossible, may become the most exciting things since sliced bread. Changes and growth in your relationship with your partner also change what is possible, exciting, and satisfying. And if and when you move on to a new partner, you will probably need to explore an entirely new spectrum of possibilities.

8.1 Yourself

When you read through these lists, think about your own reactions to the things I talk about. You may find some things intriguing, some disgusting, some terrifying, and some just plain boring.

For example, some people find blindfolds scary[3]. Blindfolds can take them well out of their comfort zone and even if they're happy to be dangled upside down while their tits are flogged, they really, really like to be able to see what's going on otherwise they start shaking or even panicking. If you find blindfolds scary, ask yourself why? Is it that seeing helps you stay in control? Is it that you don't trust your partner? Is it that you do trust your partner, but you're afraid to let go because of where it might take you and your relationship?

---

[3]Particularly bottoms tied firmly to an A-frame who discover that their top, who is warming up with a nine-foot single-tail whip, is the one wearing the blindfold!

Before I go too far with this, it's important that you realise that because something doesn't appeal to you or you find it scary, you don't have to do it just to prove something. If you are not attracted to asphyxiation, which is one of the riskier BDSM activities where your partner deliberately prevents you from being able to breath, this may simply indicate that asphyxiation isn't for you.

However, if your goal with your partner is to have a profound and intimate relationship and you realise that you avoid all BDSM activities where you'd have to completely put yourself in their hands—such as those involving mummification, blindfolds, cages, sensory deprivation, suspension bondage, etc.—then trust, or lack of it, is definitely something which is going to shape your BDSM relationship.

On the other hand, if you really enjoy being tied up but don't enjoy having sex at the same time, then possibly you are looking for some sort of emotional or physiological release rather than the actual nookie. Sometimes this might mean that explicitly non-sexual activities—such as cutting, piercing, or no-contact bondage or flogging—will be more up your alley, or whatever body part you play with, than play involving genitals.

The same person doesn't always do the same BDSM activity for the same reason. A bondage top might tie their partner one day because he feels like being creative with the restraint he imposes on his partner. On another day he might tie her up because he feels an urge to claim her and take control of her. These are very different motivations, but the same activity—namely, rope bondage—can be the way both of these different wants and needs get met. This is something to keep in mind because as you look through the activities here, there could be some which might work for you and your partner on some days or in some circumstances, and which won't work on other days or in other circumstances.

If you can't stand being given orders, perhaps you have an issue with being controlled. In this case, you might find yourself more comfortable with physical BDSM activities—such as bondage, flogging, nipple torture, etc.—than with things like humiliation, interrogation, service, and so on. Or if being of service is important to you and it's the orders themselves which don't work for you, maybe you need your partner to be clear about what they like you doing and what they don't like you doing and then you fit into that framework rather than take direct orders.

If you like serving your partner and having tasks to do for them, but only while they are in the room, then perhaps you are less a service submissive and more one who needs to feel directly and actively handled by your partner. Perhaps being on a leash, or being corset-trained, posture-trained, or micromanaged might be things which will work well for you.

If you classify yourself as a dominant but only like doing your BDSM in the form of scenes that have a clearly-defined start and end, perhaps you are more a top than a dominant.

If you are on the dominant side of the equation and you also want a profound BDSM relationship with your partner but limit yourself to light-and-fluffy BDSM games, then perhaps you either don't want or aren't ready to take responsibility... or perhaps you aren't that keen on it all anyway and are taking control just to keep your partner happy.

And if you just enjoy having your submissive partner entertain your nether regions with their tongue, then perhaps you are just a horny guy and aren't really into BDSM at all.

These are all very important reflections because what you're looking to do is have a satisfying and possibly quite profound BDSM-based relationship with your partner. Being utterly honest about what needs and wants drive you is going to go a long way towards helping that happen. If instead you let ego or pride get in the way and find yourself making a supreme effort to convincingly portray Super Dom or Supper Subbie when that isn't really what you are, then you're dooming both you and your partner to something that'll never be fully satisfying.

8.2 The lists

When you look through the lists below you will probably find many things which are limits or boundaries for you. Some people argue that you should try everything, but this is—as far as this author is concerned—a pile of doggie doo-doo. Limits are entirely reasonable things to have because the goal is not necessarily to try everything, but is instead to find those things which satisfy your own particular wants and needs. You don't need to be super kinky to be super satisfied and, in fact, if you do feel the need to try absolutely everything then it might be worth asking yourself whether this is just because you want the variety or if there's something else inside you which is preventing you from finding satisfaction.

Impact play

Impact play is where the top or dominant strikes the bottom or submissive with something. This can be with their bare hand—such as face slapping, breast slapping, or butt spanking.

Using your hand has a sense of immediacy and intimacy, particular when it's an over-the-knee spanking. There is no distance between the top and the bottom. It's up close and it's hand-to-body contact.

Many other types of impact play—such as flogging, whipping, caning, and so on—have a sense of distance associated with them. Any intimate contact must be performed separately to the main action with the whip, flogger, or cane. It's quite common for a top or dominant who is administering a flogging or caning to pause from time to time, step up close, and then touch or caress their partner, either to reassure them or to get feedback about how they are enduring the strokes.

Physical distance can be important for bottoms and submissives who use the regular, repetitive strokes to achieve a particular state of mind such as sub-space. When this is the case, personal contact can be distracting for them and can prevent them from reaching the state of mind they're after. Thus, the fact that their partner must stay out of arm's reach to use the cane, whip, or flogger is quite necessary for them.

Most forms of impact play have emotional or psychological associations which makes some types more suitable than others in particular situations. For example, if you and your partner are looking to explore impact play for a punishment scenario then caning or spanking would be good choices. On the other hand, if you're looking for some sexual overtones then breast slapping or pussy whipping would probably be more suitable.

Face slapping, whether forehand or backhand, can be associated with humiliation or with putting someone in their place, and it's definitely a statement saying, "I am in charge! Now get back to where you belong!"

When you're looking to explore or express physical domination or control then using heavier implements will be more effective than, say, slapping. Physically striking, kicking, or manhandling your partner can also carry the feeling of physically overwhelming them.

The choice of implement you use will determine the feel of the strokes and the amount of pain involved, if any. Floggers come in a range of weights with varying tail lengths. They can sting or thud, or be heavy or light. Canes often sting and then leave a burning feeling. Whips, when wielded well, can actually cut the skin and this is a very sharp pain.

Finally, heavy or intense impact play can be cathartic both for the person receiving the strokes and for the person administering them.

Some of the more common forms of impact play include:

- **Caning** - striking with a cane, or with a stiff plastic or fibreglass rod, usually on the buttocks or backs of the thighs.

- **Cropping** - striking with a riding crop.

- **Flogging** - striking or applying a multi-tail flogger, often to the upper back or buttocks. Can be sharp or dull pain.

- **Paddling** - striking a wood or leather paddle on the backside.

- **Spanking** - using your hand.

- **Spanking** - using a hairbrush.

- **Strapping** - striking with a leather belt or strap, typically to the buttocks or the backs of the thighs.

- **Whipping** - using a single-tail whip, typically to the upper back.

More specific or particular forms of impact play include:

Face slapping. We often regard our face as one of the most private parts of our body. Although we display it for everyone to see, very few people actually get to touch it. Being slapped in the face is something we usually experience as quite invasive. It can be very effective as a control-taking move by a dominant or master. Be careful not to slap near the eyes.

Back-handed face slapping is usually harder or stronger than a forehand slap, i.e., slapping with the palm of the hand. With a forehand slap the hand is extended and strikes flat with the soft, inner part of the hand. A backhand slap is usually done with the hand relaxed and the fingers curled. This allows the boney finger joints and nails to strike. A back-handed slap can be symbolic of putting someone in their place and can carry more emotional impact than a forehand slap.

Pummelling. Many forms of impact play are specific to certain parts of the body. Some people look for an assault-style of impact play, perhaps as a form of forced subjugation, and this is more of an all-body thing. It includes **kicking**, **punching**, and general **beating**. This can sometimes be combined with **wrestling**.

Pussy whipping, **breast slapping**, and **CBT** (cock and balls torture) all focus the impacts on bits of the body which we normally consider to be sexual. This can be highly symbolic and the effects quite powerful. The person doing the striking needs to be careful because these bits of the body are generally quite sensitive and damage easily.

Corporal punishment and **over-the-knee spanking** can carry with them a feeling of punishment or of being disciplined. Some people do them in a schoolroom setting or while the person being punished is in school-uniform. There can be an element of **role play** in this which can help create the right mood for this to work.

Breast slapping is, as the name suggests, slapping one or both breasts with a hand or with a paddle. This is most effective with someone with ample breasts and can be quite sexual. It can also cause bruising, and it can be quite painful due both to the impact itself and to the consequent violent bouncing of the breasts stretching the skin and pulling against ligaments.

Role play

Role play is where the two people in the scene act out roles different to their normal everyday ones. This is done for two reasons.

Firstly, the roles almost always involve a difference in authority or power. If we're talking about something like kitten play—where the submissive acts like a playful or mischievous kitten—then we have opportunities for the submissive to act up and then be chastised or punished by her master. Even when no mischievousness or punishment is involved, a kitten's owner is in an inherently more powerful position than the kitten and can choose the kitten's food, require the kitten to eat from a bowl on the floor, direct the kitten's house training, and so on.

When the two roles are human this authority or power difference can come from the age differences being played—especially when the submissive or bottom is playing an infant. This creates opportunities for humiliation such as having your diaper changed with accompanying colourful comments, having food and drink choices taken from you, being dressed or undressed, etc.

A difference in power or authority can come from other roles such as doctor and patient, police officer and prostitute, soldier and commanding officer, etc. Even though the two people involved are normally able to consent, one of the factors of many forms of role play is that consent is removed by the role. For example, in a scenario where a police officer pulls over an inebriated but pretty driver, the police officer is empowered to do things without the consent of the driver such as arrest them and handcuff them.

The second reason why role play can be effective is that it removes the two people in the scene from their normal lives and from their normal standards of behaviour. This allows them to do things, such as hit their partner, which they might not be able to readily consider when being themselves. Role play takes them away from themselves for a brief while so they can be "bad". When the role ends they feel separate from the "bad them" in the scene. This means that role play can be an effective tool to help bypass inhibitions, particularly inhibitions to do with inflicting pain on, being rough with, or disempowering your partner. Military interrogation[4], for example, is a form of role play in which you deliberately create an environment very distinct from normal life where a bottom or submissive can be tortured.

- **Age play** - adopting the role of someone much older or, more commonly, much younger. Even though the person

---

[4]Which I will mention again a little later.

playing the role is above the age of consent, the role is commonly of someone below the age of consent such as a schoolboy or schoolgirl. See below for *infantilism*.

- **Animal play** - adopting the role of an animal. Common animals are cats and kittens, dogs and puppies, and horses and ponies. There may be an element of utility in this with dogs or ponies pulling carts, being dressed up, or being trained to perform tricks.

- **Castration fantasy** - what's on the box, though some people have actually gone so far as to do it for real (in which case it can only be done once... or possibly twice).

- **Doctor and nurse** - role play of an illicit nature between consenting adults in adult roles, though with the doctor being in a position of authority over the nurse.

- **Doctor and patient** - also role play of an illicit nature between consenting adults in adult roles, though this time the doctor has an implicit rather than explicit authority to which the patient can surrender. The patient can sometimes take the dominant or initiating role by attempting, for example, to seduce the doctor. On the other hand, the doctor can also dominate and penetrate the patient with something like a catheter or other probing instrument.

- **Dressing up** - adopting the role of another person, perhaps a king, a dancing girl, a French maid, and so on.

- **Fantasy rape** - is role play where one partner is taken "against their will" and violated. See also *kidnapping* below.

- **Incest play** - adopting the role of the son or, more commonly, daughter of the dominant. Typically the son/daughter role will be in their teens to very early twenties. Might also be called **daddy/daughter play**.

- **Infantilism** - involving diapers, dummies, cots or cribs, prams and strollers, etc.

- **Kidnapping** - role play involving abduction. This can be quite complex and involve abduction from the street, bundling the victim into a car with the aid of masked friends, and so on.

- **Kitten play** - a type of *animal play* often involving a mischievous kitten which might need to be toilet trained or disciplined.

- **Pony play** - play including saddles, small carts, bridles and mouth bits, grooming, dressage, feed bags, etc.

- **Prison scenes** - role play scenes involving prisoners and warders. Might include cages, "watering down" (hosing the prisoner), and possibly escapes. Can also provide a context for *fantasy rape*.

- **Puppy play** - a type of *animal play* which can have a lot in common with *kitten play*.

- **Religious scenes** - organised religions often involve power hierarchies and/or sexual repression. Both of these are ripe for exploitation in role play. Could be a priest taking advantage of a local parishioner who has come to him or her because the parishioner has sinned, or could be something to do with a nun, etc.

Sensation play

BDSM is often about control, and while pain can be a tool for control it isn't the only physical sensation which we can inflict. Sensation play is about controlling what your partner can see, hear, feel, smell, and even taste. This can include exercises of sensory deprivation where you cover your submissive's eyes so they can't see, cover their ears so they can't hear, and wrap them in soft cloth or cotton wool so they can't feel. This can create a very powerful sense of isolation and powerlessness.

At the other end of sensation play, you can use ice or flame to create feelings of cold and heat, use scented oils and perfumes to stimulate sense of smell, use fingers or feathers to tickle, pin wheels (Wartenberg wheels) to create pricking sensations, and violet wands or T.E.N.S. units to create sparks and electrical currents in your partner's skin.

- **Abrasion** - using sandpaper, rough cloth, or coarse rope to rub against and lightly tear or abrade the skin.

- **Blindfolds** - can also be useful for someone who can't keep their eyes closed on their own, such as when they constantly want to see what's going on.

- **Ear plugs**

- **Fire cupping** - based on traditional medicine and uses round glass cups and fire. Using a small amount of volatile, flammable liquid, a small flame is lit in a cup pressed against the skin. The flame burns briefly and consumes some of the oxygen in the cup. This creates a suction effect which then holds the glass cup in place on the skin.

- **Flame/fire play** - brushing a small amount of volatile, flammable liquid on bare skin and then igniting the vapour to produce a brief flash of flame and warmth.

- **Hood** - to cover the head, ears, eyes, nose, and mouth.

- **Hot oils and spices** - applied to the body or on the genitals. Can produce pleasant or strong scents. Can also create feeling of warmth or even burning.

- **Hot wax** - dripping molten wax from candles onto the skin.

- **Hot wax** - for removing hair. The tearing-off part can hurt.

- **Ice** - can be sensual when rubbed on some parts of the skin in small amounts, such as on nipples. Can also be used to tickle or to torture someone who is tied up and who can't escape.

- **Isolation tanks** - these are closed tanks containing warm water at around body temperature. Most physical sensation is removed due to the skin's lack of contact with clothing or hard surfaces. The closed tank also minimises air movement and muffles any external sounds.

- **Lotions, potions, salves, and creams** - create sensations as they are applied, such as by massage. They may also have their own scents.

- **Padded gloves** - limit the wearer's sensation via their fingers and hands. They can also be tools to disempower the wearer because they can't effectively use their hands any more, even to remove the gloves.

- **Perfumes**

- **Scratching** - using fingernails, pins, or wooden skewers to rub against, scratch, or poke the skin.

- **Scented candles**

- **T.E.N.S. unit** - this is a device used to stimulate muscles through the skin using electricity. It is more fully known as a *Transcutaneous Electrical Nerve Stimulation* device. It creates twitching, buzzing, and pulsing feelings in the muscles.

- **Tickling** - can become torture when extreme and when combined with bondage.

- **Violet wand** - this is a device which passes high-voltage electricity at safe and low currents through a gas discharge tube (which typically glows violet, hence the name). This creates mild to strong electric shocks via sparks which jump from the glass tube to the submissive's or bottom's skin.

- **Wartenberg wheel** - a neurological testing tool consisting of a spiked wheel which is rolled across the skin. The spikes are extremely sharp, and as well as the sensation of tiny pricks these can inspire a certain amount of fear.

Bondage

Metal bondage refers to restraining someone using metal chains, cuffs, cages, and so on. The point about metal is that it's hard, cold, and immovable. Rope and leather bondage are very different because rope and leather have some flexibility and can be stretched, twisted, bent, or folded. Metal can't. This makes it attractive to people who want that feeling of inflexibility, of knowing that they can't wiggle out of the cuffs you put them in, and of knowing that they stay in the cage until you unlock it.

Here are some other points about bondage:

- There's always a bit of looseness in metal bondage. Metal cuffs are rarely snug and they allow the person wearing them some movement without the cuffs biting into them. Metal cages may even have enough room to allow moving around.

- Because of the flexibility and stretchiness of rope, some submissives see trying to escape from rope bondage as part of the exercise. In fact, for some submissives you can completely spoil the bondage experience for them by placing them in metal bondage instead of rope because metal can feel escape-proof.

- Bondage can be full-body. You can use chain or rope to tie someone head to toe. Mummification is a powerful variant on this. It uses kitchen wrap or similar to bind arms, legs, and torso into a mummy-like package.

- Bondage can also be applied just to part of the body. Hands and feet can be bound or cuffed together. Breasts and cocks can be bound with rope. You can gag your partner with cloth or tape, or you can stick a dildo in their mouth and hold it there with a strap.

Bondage can be used to control your partner. Tightly tying them, particularly when they're naked, can cause them to be helplessly sexually available and unable to resist what you do. Spreader bars, which attach to their ankles or knees and hold them apart, are also good for this. Slings and swings are webs of connected leather straps which allow you to tie your partner with their legs apart and have them suspended at your waist height so you can do very naughty things to them while comfortably standing over them.

You can tie or cage your partner and then control when they drink, when and how they go to the toilet, and what else they can do. You can suspend them upside down, put them in a straight jacket, and you decide when they get out.

Finally, in part because it uses the human body, bondage can be artistic. In the right hands, rope and chains can be placed to accentuate the shape of different parts of the body, such as the breasts, or to create intricate patterns of ropes, knots, and colours.

- **Arm/leg sleeves** - are long sleeves into which both arms or both legs are placed. The sleeves usually have laces which can be used to pull the arms or legs tightly together. Arm sleeves are often used behind a bottom's back and will hold their arms straight and rigid.

- **Breast bondage** - often used more to squeeze or press breasts than to actually restrain movement. In other words, most other forms of bondage are used to stop a person moving in some way. Breast bondage is more for sensation and is used to press the breasts in place when wrapped tightly over them, or to squeeze them when wrapped around them.

- **Cages/confinement**

- **Chains**

- **Collars** - are leather or padded steel collars typically with a number of anchor points or D-rings which can be used to attach a rope or leash, or as anchor points for a more complex bondage tie.

- **Cuffs** - handcuffs, ankles cuffs, and leg cuffs.

- **Decorative bondage** - is a type of rope bondage where there is a focus on the colour, symmetry, or pattern of the ropes and knots. The actual restraining ability of the tie may be secondary.

- **Finger bondage** - restraining just fingers. For example, spreading out the fingers of one hand and then tying each individual finger to the one chopstick. Also the Chinese finger trap.

- **Gags** - cloth gags, inflatable gags, phallic gags, rubber gags, tape gags, or underwear or stockings stuffed in the mouth.

- **Genital bondage** - typically used for guys, for obvious reasons. Can be used to squeeze or as a way of stopping them running away[5] in the manner of a leash. Some forms of rope bondage, particularly those involving a rope harness (see next item), have a rope passing between the legs of the bottom, in which case an opportunely placed knot can be very effective for both males and females.

- **Harnesses** - these are made of leather or tied with rope and are typically used as anchor points for further bondage. A harness usually doesn't restrict movement, but like on a horse or other animal a harness gives you places to which you can attach other things. A full-body rope

---

[5] As if they would!

harness, for example, is often a prerequisite for suspension bondage because it can give good body support and provide multiple points to which you can tie the ropes or chains to suspend the bottom.

- **Hog tie** - for complete immobilisation. Be careful doing this on someone with flexibility problems.

- **Intricate bondage** - a variant on decorative bondage where the fine detail is important. Finer ropes and cords may be used in intricate bondage.

- **Japanese rope bondage** - more specific type or subset of decorative bondage often using particular ropes, stances or positions, and knots.

- **Manacles and irons** - heavy and onerous to wear around. These really give the feeling of being restrained.

- **Mummification, plastic wrapping** - using plastic kitchen wrap to bind arms, legs, or the whole body. Overheating is a serious risk, as is suffocation if the wrap is too tight over the chest.

- **Nipple bondage** - specifically on nipples only and completely separate to breast bondage. Uses fine cord, shoe laces, string, fishing line, etc.

- **Posture frames and braces** - these hold a submissive's head or back firmly in one position while still allowing them to move around. High heels for someone unfamiliar with wearing them can have a similar effect (such as on some guys).

- **Slings** - these are webs of leather straps, often suspended horizontally or near-horizontally, to which a submissive or bottom can be tied and then explored (i.e., sexually) or flogged.

- **Spreader bars** - rods which attach to cuffs on the ankles or knees which hold the legs apart to expose the genitals.

- **Stocks** - two pieces of hinged wood which, when closed and locked, have three holes. One large one in the middle for the head, and two on either side of this for the wrists or, with someone flexible, the ankles. Stocks can be fixed, such as being on a heavy stand, or "wearable".

- **Straight jacket**

- **Suspension bondage** - tying someone and suspending them above the ground. Can be horizontal suspension bondage (i.e., body horizontal, face up or face down), upside-down bondage, or vertical bondage.

- **Thumb cuffs** - miniature metal, lockable cuffs which fit around the base of the thumbs. Very similar to handcuffs, though obviously much smaller.

Objectification

Controlling your partner, if that's what turns you on, isn't just ordering them around or forcing them to kiss your feet. An important part of some people's BDSM is the objectification of their partner. This controls the partner's feelings of self-worth or even their feeling of being human. Lending your submissive to another dominant without asking your submissive first is treating them as a possession or as an object. Likewise, requiring your submissive to pose as a statue, or using them as a toilet, is dehumanising them. These are all strong statements that you control your submissive's value.

Sometimes objectification is an attempt to humiliate or dehumanise, but some submissives can find it an exciting and powerful opportunity to serve their partner by being, say, the best candleholder in the room. For some this might sound funny, but it is a difficult goal to achieve as it requires staying motionless for long periods. There are submissives who relish such forms of challenge posed by their partner.

- **Being auctioned** - this is sometimes a BDSM party game where submissives are auctioned off for the evening to the highest-bidding dominant. This can be simply a bit of fun because usually what happens in such a situation is that the submissive gets tied up or flogged in front of others at the party by the winning dominant. It becomes more serious, and more penetrating, when the winning dominant gets to take the submissive for a day or a weekend with few limits.

- **Being given away or loaned** - similar to being auctioned, but in this case the owner dominant gives or loans out his submissive to another dominant. This reinforces the idea that the submissive is property and has few rights.

- **Being inspected** - treating a submissive like a car or horse and inspecting her ("it") as if they were an object whose feelings do not need to be regarded, particularly when the dominant performing the inspection comments or rates different aspects of the submissive to another dominant as he does so. This can be very objectifying.

- **Being used as furniture** - as a chair, table, candleholder, door prop, towel holder, etc.

The lists

- **Serving as art** - posing as a statue or modelling.

- **Being used as a toilet or chamber pot**

Pain play and torture

In BDSM, pain is used to achieve a goal. This goal could be sub-space, catharsis, an assuaging of guilt, increased sexual arousal, or greater intimacy. We can distinguish this from true sadism which, depending on the definition you use, has to do with sexual fantasies, urges, or behaviour; or which has to do with simply getting a thrill out of seeing someone else in pain. There's typically a sense of selfishness in true sadism where the goal is to hurt for one's own pleasure. In BDSM, apart from it often not being about sex at all, when pain is used it is usually more about healing than hurting, and it's about being mutually beneficial and satisfying as opposed to being just selfish.

It's notable that when we're looking at activities where you directly seek out the experience of pain, one of the key ideas is suffering. The pain needs to be suffered or endured to be effective. This is the case with catharsis, for example, or with assuaging guilt. One of the problems with pain though, is that many bottoms and submissives will reach a certain pain level and will then either slip into sub-space or else their body will start releasing endorphins and the pain becomes muted. The pain stops being felt. In particular this can happen when the pain is spread over a large area and becomes overwhelming, such as when the whole of the back is used during flogging.

There's nothing wrong with sub-space, of course; it is often a desirable outcome. But when the goal is to suffer the pain and sub-space occurs instead then the aimed-for goal simply isn't achieved. You might have been on the road to a fine catharsis, but then your body and mind swerved, and you ended up in sub-space or a neurochemical high instead.

The list here is about directly causing pain and suffering. In all cases, for pain or torture to be effective it needs to be and remain focussed. Physical pain needs to focus on one part of the body. Nipples are always excellent because they can be quite sensitive. A woman's clitoris or a man's cock or testicles are also localised enough to be effective. Using a knife and cutting patterns into the skin will be most effective when only a small area is cut rather than if you were to cut designs all over your poor submissive's entire front or back.

Suffering can also come from forced lack of sleep or from forced sexual deprivation (the well-known "blue balls").

- **Biting** - nipples or other loose flesh.

- **CBT** (cock and ball torture) - ball stretching, clamping, piercing, pegging, nailing, or crushing.

- **Clothespegs or clamps** - attached to different or interesting parts of the body such as testicles, nipples, lips (on the face, and lower down on the ladies), the back, earlobes, and so on. Don't leave on too long because they restrict blood flow.

- **Cutting** - using a scalpel or hobby knife to cut into the skin.

- **Nipple clamps** - applying special clamps to one or more nipples. There are a variety of clamps specially designed for this. The amount of squeeze pressure usually can be adjusted.

- **Nipple torture** - inflicting pain on nipples using tight clamps, pins, pinching, or twisting.

- **Nipple weights** - attaching clamps to nipples and then hanging weights from the clamps. Best done while the submissive is tied and leaning forward.

- **Pinching**

- **Scratching** - using sharp fingernails or metal objects with sharp points to scratch sensitive skin. The belly is good for this.

- **Sexual deprivation**

- **Sleep deprivation**

- **Water torture**

- **Whipping** - the tip of a well-cracked whip can be travelling at supersonic speed. It can cut or sting.

- **Zipper** - an exercise involving a line of clothes-pegs clipped to the pinched-up skin of a submissive. Through the line of pegs is threaded a string. When the string is quickly pulled, the clothespegs are pulled off the skin in rapid succession, hence "zipper". Fun for all ages.

Control and authority

Exploration of power—either using it on your partner or having them use it on you—is a common desire or need for people into BDSM. It can be done through physical activities expressly intended to create a feeling of one person having more control or power than the other such as bondage or pain play. You can also cut straight to the chase and simply take control of your partner during everyday activities regardless of where or when they do them. In some ways this can be more intense than BDSM scenes involving rope or dungeons or floggers. Anything done in a scene is going to be effective only for the duration of the scene. There's a built-in escape clause—when the scene ends, the control ends. Instead, when you take control of everyday activities, there is no sense of when the control is going to end. There is no possibly-reassuring feeling that it's going to end soon and that you can go back to being in full control again. This sense and awareness of control can become a constant all-day part of life. Indeed, for some this is, in fact, quite comforting and reassuring.

Any part of life is fair game for this sort of control. It can be what clothes to wear—which can be as simple as before dressing the submissive or slave must lay out the clothes they think they should wear that day and wait for their master to change or approve their choice; or it can be what food to eat and when—such as being required to wait until master has taken his first bite of food or first sip of drink before the submissive can do the same; or it can be how the submissive cuts or wears their hair, what make-up they wear, how they speak to or address their master, and so on.

Importantly, this is not a one-way exercise. It requires the dominant or master to claim the authority and use it. It isn't sufficient to give an order just once and then expect the submissive to feel happy and content forever more without any further contribution from the dominant. This is unsatisfying for both. Meaningfully having authority involves wielding that authority, making choices, and ensuring compliance.

The lists

Some areas of control have to do with self-expression and identity. It's useful to recognise that these can have markedly different effects on both the submissive and dominant when compared to more impersonal control. For example, directing how a submissive should wear their hair or what clothes they wear is going to have more of a personal impact than if you direct them to always walk on your left or to order the salad instead of the burger. The former has to do with identity, while the latter is behaviour.

Anything to do with controlling or restricting someone's opportunities for expressing themselves sexually, or for satisfying themselves sexually, can also strike deeply at their sense of self. This can be particularly powerful.

- **Asphyxiation** - also known as breath play, this involves restricting or controlling the breathing of a submissive. One way this is done is to use a mask similar to a World War II gas mask which has valves to control the air flow. Asphyxiation can also include strangulation. Sometimes asphyxiation is used to intensify orgasm, but is obviously quite dangerous and, at times, deadly.

- **Code of behaviour** - this is when a dominant or master imposes standards or rules of behaviour on their submissive. This can include how they address their partner, how they dress, how they behave in public and in private, and so on.

- **Chastity devices** - these devices are used to control when someone can have sex. For females, these can be like lockable metal panties which prevent anything substantial entering their cunt, while for males they will be lockable enclosures for their cocks.

- **Collar and leash** - this involves leading a submissive around like a pet.

- **Competitions with other submissives** - such as the famous peanut race where a row of naked submissives are each compelled to push a peanut pod or shell (still containing the peanuts) along a course with their nose. Imagine the view from behind! Also, competitions for who can kneel the smoothest, who can remain stationary the longest, etc.

- **Dress code** - setting standards of dress (or undress) for a submissive or slave.

- **Eye contact restrictions** - these are restrictions imposed on a submissive by their dominant, typically that the submissive must keep their eyes lowered to the floor when they are addressing their dominant unless told otherwise.

- **Food or eating control** - restrictions or limits on what a submissive or slave may eat and when. As well as affecting choice of how much to eat, sometimes this is used when a submissive dines with their dominant partner to determine when the submissive may eat or drink (e.g., only after their dominant has begun to eat or drink), or when they must end their meal (e.g., when their dominant lays down his or her cutlery or napkin). A submissive may also be sent to bed without their supper as a punishment.

- **Following orders**

- **Forced feminization** - a male submissive or slave being compelled to wear women's clothing, underwear, or makeup.

- **Forced homosexuality** - for entrenched heterosexual submissives.

- **Forced heterosexuality** - for entrenched homosexual submissives.

- **Forced masturbation** - particularly in front of an audience, this can be quite effective for a timid or self-conscious submissive of either gender.

- **Forced nudity** - in private, or in the presence of others, e.g., at a BDSM party or social event.

- **Forced orgasm** - often with the submissive bound so they can't escape the stimulation.

- **Forced servitude**

- **Hair pulling** - grabbing a submissive by the hair, particularly the hair on the back of their head, can be a powerful way of taking control of their head. This can then be used to manipulate them, or to push them into particular positions such as onto their knees.

- **Having clothing chosen for you** - for a submissive this can involve not being allowed to dress in the morning until their dominant has chosen the clothes they will be wearing. The submissive doesn't get to choose at all, including not choosing their underwear (or lack of it).

- **Having food chosen for you** - it's important to distinguish between controlling the manner in which a submissive or slave eats, as mentioned above in *food or eating control*, and controlling or choosing what they eat or drink. At restaurants, for example, the dominant may choose what the submissive can order or, more generally, may claim overall control over the submissive's diet.

- **Manhandling** - is a very primal expression of dominance and of claiming and asserting control at a very base, animal level. Grabbing someone, pushing them to the ground, manhandling them into a position, physically undressing them, dragging them by the hair, and so on, are all very primal acts.

- **Mouth soaping** - as a punishment this is a classic. It can bring back memories of childhood. It can also be humiliating.

- **Orgasm control** - this usually refers to limiting when and where a submissive can orgasm. It can also extend to control over masturbation.

- **Orgasm denial** - this is a more scene-oriented and immediate form of orgasm control, typically physically arousing a submissive to near the point of orgasm but not letting them get there for an extended period of time. This is usually combined with bondage.

- **Partner swapping** - when combined with sex this can be a powerful statement of authority through the dominant choosing who can have sex or play BDSM-wise with the submissive, and by the dominant allowing themselves additional BDSM or sexual partners. The sex need not be actual sexual intercourse, but anything intimate which is normally associated with sex—such as fondling, masturbation, digital penetration, or oral sex—can be fair game here.

- **Posture training** - this can be a form of bondage, but in the control-and-authority context it has more to do with the dominant directing how the submissive or slave walks, stands, kneels, or serves, with a particular focus on posture and movement.

- **Sexual deprivation** - is different to orgasm control or denial which allow the submissive or slave to become sexually aroused but usually don't allow them to climax until the frustration is painful. Instead, sexual deprivation is not allowing them any sexual stimulation at all. Chastity devices can help with this, but denying them access to porn, not allowing them to see their dominant naked, cold showers, and other strategies also help keep that particular genie in the bottle.

- **Slave name** - giving a slave or submissive a new name different to their civil name can be quite objectifying. In their mind, it can establish a slave or submissive identity separate to their day-to-day life. Because the dominant gives the slave or submissive this name they also own and control the name.

- **Speech restrictions** - limiting when and how a submissive or slave may speak can be an effective form of control. One common technique is to require the submissive or slave to refer to themselves in the third person, e.g., "This girl is very tired, master." Other rules can include that the submissive may not interrupt their dominant or must not speak until spoken to.

- **Standing orders** - these are orders from the dominant which the submissive or slave carries around with them, even when their dominant is not there. For example:

- Always ensuring that the car is filled with gas when they bring it home,
- Making sure the refrigerator is always stocked with the dominant's favourite drinks,
- Ensuring that the beds are always made before 9am on weekdays,
- Making sure that the apartment is always dusted twice per week,
- The submissive must always have their shoes shined, or
- The submissive must always greet the dominant at the door.

- **Wrestling** - like manhandling, wrestling can be a primal expression which signals the dominant's dominance over the submissive (especially, of course, if the dominant wins).

Worship

Many BDSM activities involve one person—such as the dominant—doing something to create a change in feelings or sensations, or doing something to restrain or impose pain on their partner. These are concrete changes caused by the interaction of the dominant with the submissive. On the other hand, some forms of BDSM play are more symbolic or ritualistic and the pleasure comes less from the actual interaction between the two people involved and more from their internal reaction to it.

Worship is one such form. It is often highly symbolic and can require specific posturing by one or both partners, a specific context, and can even require specific clothing. It can be a ritualistic enactment of a difference in power involving the submissive or slave lowering themselves in some way—from bowing down or kneeling, to kissing or licking the boots of their partner. Boot cleaning, even in the absence of the partner's feet in said boots can also be included here. This lowering or abasing can be in relation to the whole dominant or in relation to some specific part of their body, such as their foot, or especially their cock or cunt.

- **Cock worship** - kneeling or lowering oneself in front of the dominant's cock, or lavishing attention on the dominant's cock.

- **Foot worship** - kneeling and possibly kissing the dominant's foot or shoe.

- **High heel worship** - ditto, but for high heels. High heels often have a special symbolism. Beyond sometimes being fetish objects, they are often perceived as powerful statements of being female and so the worship can be both of the dominant (or their shoes) and of femaleness in general.

- **Kneeling** - lowering and abasing oneself at the feet of your partner. The posture can be important in this because lowering your head completely to the ground, e.g., forehead on the ground, is different to kneeling upright. The latter might be an attentive position of readiness more than worship.

- **Licking boots** - this can involve symbolism in a number of ways. Firstly, boots can be seen as trampling tools. They press down or squash what's beneath them. Secondly, they usually aren't sexual. Instead, they are strictly, and often brutally, utilitarian and everyone is equal before them. Thirdly, licking can be symbolic of taking the boots into oneself, of being penetrated by them physically. Finally, they are the lowest part of the dominant and, as with any form of worship involving feet or shoes, they require lowering one's self to the level of, or below, the lowest part of the dominant.

- **Pussy worship** - like cock worship... well, not exactly like, but the intention and the result can be similar. It is worth comparing pussy and cock worship which are specifically genital-focused, and something like high-heel worship which is gender-focused.

- **Rituals** - such as bowing the head when entering the room, backing out of rooms so as not to turn your back on your dominant, etc.

Sexual play

Sexual play between two people provides many opportunities for one to do various things to their partner to arouse, stimulate, objectify, make them feel vulnerable, humiliate, or sexually control them in some way. In BDSM, this is often done in combination with other activities such as bondage. Sex itself is often a very intense and powerful experience anyway, and adding in BDSM elements can make it more so. All of the activities listed here lend themselves to being given a BDSM twist, as well as most of them being potentially very sexually arousing in their own right.

- **Anal beads** - a string of beads inserted where the Sun don't shine. Rather than their presence creating interesting feelings as with something like a dildo, it is more the sensations as they are inserted and, specifically, removed which make them interesting.

- **Anal plugs** - these are devices which block up the rear passage. These can range from small to quite large, the latter requiring some training to accommodate. They are usually shaped so that once in they tend to stay in place. The part which remains outside the body is commonly flat, and the person with the anal plug inserted may be able to sit or walk around with it in place.

- **Anal sex**

- **Breast fucking** - cock-between-tits sex. Of course, this requires large-ish breasts. For the owner of the tits, this can also be objectifying.

- **Chastity devices** - making them wait until you get home.

- **Dildos**

- **Double penetration** - two holes for the price of one! For threesomes, or for two people where one has a possibly-vibrating friend.

- **Fisting** - using a suitably lubricated hand to go in orifices not originally intended for it. As well as creating strong feelings of penetration objectively, there can be a lot of surrender associated with the process (which typically takes a fair while to perform to achieve stretching rather than tearing).

- **Fucking machine** - electrically-powered thrusting devices. Never get tired. Always in the mood. Don't roll over and go to sleep before you've climaxed. These are sometimes used as devices of sexual torture by dominants who want to overload their submissive sexually while remaining in control of the action more than if their own genitals were also involved.

- **Gang bang** - one submissive, many dominants. Or, one female, many males. The singleton is the target of the sexual attentions of the others.

- **Genital sex** - one on one, genital-to-genital sex. This is not exciting AT ALL and is just mentioned here for completeness.

- **Group sex** - multiple submissives, multiple dominants. Or, multiple females and multiple males. No holes barred.

- **Hand jobs and masturbation**

- **Oral sex** - there can be some overlap between oral sex and cock or pussy worship. E.g., the "benefit" for the receiver can be straight sexual pleasure while for the giver it can be worship.

- **Outdoor sex**

- **Phone sex**

- **Rimming** - using your tongue to explore and stimulate your partner's anus.

- **Rough sex** - sex involving lots of physical force and manhandling. This can be an expression of dominance and submission, and of asserting control. See also *Manhandling* on page 146).

- **Sex during menstruation** - there can be a lot of symbolism here, particularly to do with femaleness.

- **Strap-on dildo** - a power statement by a female allowing her to sexually dominate a male or female partner. This can also include an aspect of cock worship.

- **Swinging** - also known as partner swapping. Switching back to a discussion on relationships for a moment here, partner swapping and swinging are often more about penetration (often literally) than engagement.

- **Talking dirty**

- **Triple penetration** - three holes in play at once. Usually only women are qualified for this.

- **Vibrating egg** - a type of vibrator which is used internally. There are two ways for women to use this, and one for men. One interesting advantage of these is that they are applied internally and so can be used in public. In D&s terms, a remote-controlled vibrator can allow a dominant to sexually stimulate his submissive silently and from a distance, leaving them to deal with the arousal. Can be a type of sexual torture.

- **Vibrator** - the externally-applied variety. These can get quite powerful, in which case they require habituation (getting used to).

In a lot of cases, the activities and devices mentioned above are suitable for one partner (the dominant) to use on their partner (the submissive) with the intent of expressing control over them, dominating them, and objectifying or humiliating them.

Medical play

With penetration—namely, the importance of you feeling your partner and their reactions, and of them feeling yours—being a vital part of actually having a relationship, the ability to open yourself up, let down your barriers and defences and allow your partner in is key. While actual sexual intercourse and some types of BDSM play—such as cutting and piercing—do involve physical penetration, medical play can take this to the maximum extent possible by using medical equipment and procedures to physically penetrate the body of a submissive profoundly and intimately.

- **Blood play** is any form of BDSM play where blood is intentionally released. This can apply to heavy impact play, cutting, piercing, and so on. This can be very symbolic.

- **Catheterization** - this is really, seriously, and definitely an activity which should only be practised by people with the appropriate medical training such as doctors and nurses. It involves inserting probes into such places as your urethra. Inserted far enough the person holding the catheter has control over your peeing.

- **Dental or oral play**

- **Dilation** - making little body holes into big body holes using stretching devices. Oral, vaginal, and anal. As well as being symbolic, these can cause strong physical sensations of being penetrated.

- **Douches**

- **Enemas**

- **Examinations** - medical-type examinations can be both objectifying and humiliating, depending on how they're done. Treating a submissive like meat, or by performing a protracted examination in very fine detail (with verbal comments), particularly of some part of their body about which they are sensitive, can be very effective. Don't forget to keep your speculum in the refrigerator before use!

- **Injections** - also inadvisable for people who don't have medical training. However, when injections are done in BDSM they are often a saline (inert) solution which has no medical effect. They can cause pain depending on the needle bore.

- **Lactation** - play involving milking breasts.

- **Speculums** - for probing bodily orifices.

Service

Service is where a submissive or slave attends to the wants, needs, or orders of their partner. In terms of disparity of power, it is highly representative, with the dominant providing the wants, needs, and orders without which the submissive will have nothing to do and no way to find satisfaction or pleasure.

Service can be personal or impersonal. In BDSM it is most commonly personal because many submissives get a large part of their satisfaction from directly interacting with and pleasing their dominant, i.e., from seeing their dominant being pleased.

Running errands, going out and paying bills, doing shopping, and so forth, are not particularly personal and there isn't much opportunity for the necessary feedback for those submissives who need it.

Different forms of service can have different amounts of personal-ness in them. Sexual service can be highly personal. Attending master's table as a waitress is less so, while being master's chauffeur can be almost completely impersonal.

- **Chores** - housework, washing dishes, cleaning, vacuuming, dusting, washing and hanging out clothes.

- **Home handyman(woman)** - household repairs, changing tap washers, painting, oiling squeaky hinges, carrying heavy objects, replacing light bulbs, minor electrical repairs, minor carpentry, minor car servicing duties (changing oil, charging flat battery, etc.)

- **Errands** - shopping, carrying parcels, delivering messages, paying bills, fetching things.

- **Massage -** sexual or non-sexual.

- **Chauffeur** - driving master or mistress around, cleaning and polishing the car, carrying parcels to and from the car, delivering parcels and letters, taking the car to be serviced.

- **Serving as waiter or waitress** - setting the table, taking food or drink orders, serving food and drinks, waiting attentively during meals, taking away dishes, glasses, and cutlery at the end of each course, serving dessert.

- **Serving as cook** - planning meals ahead of time, preparing or cooking meals.

- **Serving as gardener** - gardening, weeding, mowing the lawn, potting, fertilising, planning and maintaining a vegetable garden, planning and planting seasonal flowers.

- **Serving other dominants** - providing any of the above to other dominants under the direction of your dominant.

Psychological play

Much of the time in BDSM we use physical activities such as flogging, bondage, service, and so forth, to create changed awareness or sensations. This allows one person to control or direct the experience of the other. This experience is then used internally to achieve some productive outcome, be it a feeling of security, catharsis, orgasm, or whatever. This is a little indirect because while we might inflict a painful flogging, it doesn't guarantee that we'll get the desired outcome such as sub-space, but may just get instead howls of pain and cries of, "You bastard!"

In psychological play, the goal is not so much to create a situation which the submissive or bottom uses to achieve a state of mind, but is instead to go directly towards the desired state of mind or goal via specially chosen activities. This can put the dominant in the driver's seat instead of them being simply the engine as is the case sometimes.

- **Exhibitionism** - being exposed in front of others. This could be by being partly or completely naked, or by having some hidden aspect of the submissive exposed such as wearing a BDSM collar in public or in front of friends who previously didn't know about this BDSM proclivity.

- **Outdoor scenes** - doing BDSM in the outdoors, such as in a secluded or not-so-secluded forest location, in a city early in the morning or late at night, in public under the cover of darkness, and so on. The fear of being seen or discovered can be quite penetrating.

- **Golden showers** - being pissed on.

- **Humiliation** - public and private, verbal humiliation, insults. The exhibitionism mentioned above can be a source of humiliation.

- **Hypnosis**

- **Interrogation** or, especially, military interrogation. This can be a time when the submissive is actively supposed to resist either their dominant, or the pain or torture their dominant is inflicting on them. For some submissives this can be about being taken to and beyond their breaking point, while for others it can specifically be about resisting and not being broken.

- **Wearing lingerie** - particularly if a butch or a guy.

- **Public exposure**

- **Standing in the corner** - punishment after being bad.

- **Teasing and mocking** - a variety of humiliation.

Marking

Usually, the way we look and the way we present ourselves to others is something which we use to express ourselves. It is one of the ways we say, this is who I am. When someone else, a dominant or master, takes control of an aspect of this it can be a powerful surrendering of oneself. You can find very deep surrender in the situation where someone else has the power or authority to decide when or if you get a tattoo, how to have your hair cut, what clothes you wear, and any body markings you'll have through scarification, piercing, cutting, or even branding. And when the body changes or marks are permanent—such as with a tattoo or a brand—this is a powerful statement about your commitment to the relationship or the lifestyle.

Having said that, it's clear that some forms of body marking are temporary and can be effective in scenes between two people. For example, wearing make-up can be very short-term and is a useful tool in forced feminization. Longer-term body changes can include haircuts or shaving (or not shaving), and can include dye or henna tattoos—which may last for days or weeks. Some forms of cutting can also leave scars which will heal completely over time, though this can be a bit unpredictable and will vary from person to person.

Piercing the flesh with a needle and leaving jewellery threaded through the holes is a permanent form of marking which can later be removed. Common areas for this include the ears, lips, eyebrows, tongue, nipples, navel, cock, clitoris, and labia.

- **Body decoration**

- **Branding** - this can be hot branding, typically with a red-hot wire, or cold branding with a metal template chilled with dry ice or similar. This is permanent marking. It is also quite dangerous to perform and requires a lot of skill to avoid burns which may need hospital treatment.

- **Haircut**

- **Makeup**

- **Piercing**

- **Scarification** - deliberately creating scars, often in particular shapes or designs, either through burning or through cutting, and then ensuring the wounds won't invisibly heal, such as by using tape to hold them open.

- **Shaving**, particularly the pubic area.

- **Tattooing** with ink (permanent).

- **Tattoos** with henna (temporary).

Fetishes

Strictly speaking, fetishes aren't BDSM because they're typically done solo. In any case, this book is about relationships and someone who gets turned on by the stockings or shoes that another person is wearing isn't engaged in any sort of relationship with that person. They're being turned on by the stockings, shoes, or whatever.

However, BDSM is often about power or the use of power, and fetishes can be quite powerful. Because of this, fetishes can find a place in a BDSM relationship as a tool which a dominant can use to control their fetish-susceptible partner. For example, a woman dominant whose male partner has a stocking fetish can wear stockings and let her partner touch them as a reward for good behaviour, or not wear them as a punishment for bad behaviour. Likewise, a boot fetishist can be rewarded with a fine pair of their master's or mistress' boots to polish, or can be punished by being forced to leave them uncleaned.

Material - cloth, texture, smell

- **Lace**

- **Latex**
- **Leather**
- **Nylon**
- **PVC**
- **Rubber**
- **Satin**
- **Silk**
- **Spandex**

Clothing

- **Corsets**
- **Panties**
- **Pantyhose**
- **Underwear** - clean or soiled
- **Boots**
- **High heels**
- **Cross dressing** - wearing clothing typical of the opposite sex

Parts of the body

- **Feet**

- **Elbows**

- **Hair**

Miscellaneous

- **Lactation**

- **Pregnancy**

- **Small people** - dwarves and midgets

- **Uniforms** - can be associated with power, such as nurse, doctor, or police officer

8.3   Conclusion

When you're considering any BDSM activity, and especially when you're looking through the lists above, try to think about each one from the following perspectives:

- Engagement. Is this something which will be better, more exciting, or more satisfactory when your partner is actively involved? Maybe. Contrariwise, many people like to lose themselves in their BDSM experiences and trying to engage them too much (or even at all) can be distracting.

- Penetration. How penetrating does it need to be? Too much pain, too many sensations, or even too many ropes can be overwhelming at times. Sometimes being subtle is the right approach. On the other hand, for someone looking for a lot of pain, hitting them with a small flogger can just be annoying.

- Effect on your relationship. Is this activity something which is going to help build your relationship? Is it going to help you and your partner be more intimate together? Is it going to build trust? Is it an act of sharing?

- Which wants or needs do these activities satisfy? They don't need to be profound needs such as surrender, but can be something you do just for fun, a bit of variety, or as foreplay for something else (which need not be sex). However, if the needs or wants being addressed are important, such as surrender or catharsis, then treating them lightly or as just a bit of fun can mean they don't get met at all, or that you or your partner will put up defensive barriers, and that can have a major impact on the longevity of your relationship.

Chapter 9

Maintaining balance

Before continuing, I think it's worth reflecting for a moment on balance.

The names we give to the different roles in BDSM—such as top and bottom, submissive and dominant, and master and slave—suggest that these roles are complementary. The idea is that one completes the other, that each gets their wants and needs met through their relationship with their partner. It's implicit that when they get together that they each do their thing, and when they're done all is right with the world and everyone's happy. For example, when a dominant flogs his submissive he may be satisfying his need to control and arouse his partner both through his choice of implements and through the pace and strength of the strokes he applies. Simultaneously, his submissive is surrendering and opening themselves up to the handling, the control, and the manipulation of their sexual feelings by their partner. These are entirely different needs being met, but the fact that they can be satisfied in one particular scene or activity makes them complementary. Each partner gets exactly what they want and need, and they get it in the right amount.

Well... that's the theory.

This balance isn't always the case. Sometimes the needs of a top, dominant, or master won't be in proportion to those of their submissive, bottom, or slave. When one is fully satisfied, the other may still be "hungry". This lack of balance may be a matter of degree, such as a top being satisfied after inflicting a certain amount of pain while their bottom is still wanting more pain than they have so far received.

Sometimes this lack of balance has nothing to with degree. What one person wants or needs may have no complement for their partner. For example, for some submissives the tight embrace of the rope in bondage can give them a powerful physiological release. This has nothing to do with their partner. All these submissives need is that they get tightly tied up and then are left quietly to "soak" for fifteen minutes or so. They can't do this on their own for practical and safety reasons and so a trusted top or dominant needs to do it for them. The top then sits back, has a coffee for 15 minutes while keeping an eye on the submissive, and then comes back and unties them.

Another activity which may have no complement is cutting. Some bottoms and submissives simply need the sharp pain from cutting without any form of engagement with their partner. Like the bondage example above, this tends to be a very one-way activity, with the person being bound or cut getting their needs met while their partner simply serves as a source of knots or as a wielder of the blade.

Because of this lack of balance, it can be that one of you sometimes doesn't get out of a scene what you put into it. In a longer-term relationship this can be OK because even though you might not get your own needs met in every single scene, over time you do as you each take turns to focus on what the other needs.

Lack of balance is neither a good thing nor a bad thing. It simply is. All relationships will have times when one person's wants or needs are stronger or harder to satisfy than their partner's. What is important is that you and your partner talk openly about these times and come up with strategies to handle them. This need not be or become a big issue, but it is a useful topic for discussion with your partner. Ask them how they feel about what you do together and whether their needs are getting met as part of the natural exchange of effort and energy which occurs between you both. If not, or if you feel your needs aren't getting properly met, talk about it and see what can be done.

Chapter 10

Online BDSM

From the earliest days of computer networks, even before The Internet, BDSM enthusiasts have used their computers to communicate with each other. Early bulletin board systems were accessed using dial-up modems which allowed people within the same geographical area, such as the same town or city, to post notices or announcements, or to contribute to discussions with like-minded BDSM folk.

As the reach of computer networks became regional, then national, and then international, the software and communication protocols expanded to allow this same sharing at national and international levels and distances.

In the 60s, 70s, and 80s, BDSM was very much a taboo subject and so the anonymity of both distance and screen nicknames allowed BDSM folk far and near to comfortably and safely get together electronically in huge numbers.

Early communications were in a form similar to email which could take up to a day or longer to arrive. Interactive chat soon followed which allowed people to type messages on their computer, and these would then show up on the screens of other enthusiasts within seconds of the ENTER key being pressed. This has led to "chat rooms" and on-line communities where people meet and move from one discussion to another entirely via their computer. In more recent times, this has been augmented by the ability to see and speak with others via the Internet using webcams and microphones.

Because of these new opportunities for people to interact via their computer, and because BDSM is a type of interaction between people, it should not be surprising that some people have BDSM relationships or engage in BDSM activities entirely on-line, frequently without ever having met their partner in person.

There are advantages and disadvantages to these sorts of relationships.

For people who are living in isolated areas, such contacts allow them to stay in touch with what's happening in the rest of the world, to have chats and discussions with other like-minded folk, and even to express themselves as a submissive or dominant and for their long-distance correspondent to openly respond to this.

With the addition of a little imagination it's possible to have deeper BDSM engagements. Where the communication is text-based, this sort of interaction frequently takes the form of each person describing how they are responding, or how they imagine themselves to be responding, to what their partner is writing. At the same time, the partner is also reacting in turn, and they write that back.

For people who have little or no experience with BDSM, or for those lacking the opportunities to find like-minded others in real-life, on-line BDSM can provide a safe, exciting, and anonymous environment in which to begin experimenting with BDSM.

A big disadvantage, of course, is that you're on your own when all this is happening. Real human touch is missing. Also, because the person at the other end of the computer connection is often only words on a screen, some fairly heavy imagining might be needed to create the whole picture—such as what they look like, what they're wearing, how they sound, how they move, what they say, etc. This can be difficult, both to achieve in the first place and to maintain in the longer term.

Online BDSM is also usually anonymous so you won't really have a chance to get an intimate awareness of the other person. And because it's anonymous they may disappear at any time and you won't have any idea of where they went.

10.1 Making it work

The more you have to imagine, the less satisfying it is than interacting with someone actually in front of you. The solution is to communicate a lot. Don't just send messages back and forth though. Make an effort to fill in any gaps so that less imagination is required by your partner. Likewise, ask them questions so you need less imagination to "see" them. Perhaps send pictures, not just of you, but of the room you're in, the computer you're using, the rest of the house or apartment, the area near you, and even the clothes you wear. Discuss the things that are going on in your life, talk about your friends.

Consider meeting up. This can be risky, of course, but if they're somewhere you can visit—even if just for a day—it might be worthwhile. The risk is that when you meet there won't be any magic. Or they may have been lying to you and instead of looking like Mr or Miss International they look more like Mr or Miss Short-'n-Ugly.

Ultimately, if all you and your Internet partner have together is the ability to imagine almost anything then even you are irrelevant to your partner because they can easily imagine a new partner. To engage each other—your real selves—and to be significant to each other there must be an effort on each of your parts to extend the relationship so that more than just what happens on the computer is involved.

So, talk and share. Otherwise, what you have is likely to be unsatisfying in the long-term.

Chapter 11

Here's the thing

One of the things I've noticed about many BDSM folk is that when they start talking about BDSM they'll conclude by saying something like, "Every BDSM relationship is different," or "If you take a hundred BDSM couples, you'll have a hundred different relationships." Rather than stating these simply as facts—which they are, by the way—they're using them as excuses so they don't have to look any further, effectively saying that if all these relationships are different then there's no point in trying to understand them, categorise them, or find things they have in common because they're all *different*.

This is another pile of doggie doo-doo. It may well be that understanding BDSM relationships is hard, or challenging, or maybe just not particularly obvious, but as we've seen in this book—particularly in chapter 6, *Motivations*, and in chapter 8, *The lists*—when we detach ourselves and step back enough so we can see what's actually going on, then *what it is that we do* starts to come into focus as part of a single big picture rather than as fragments of hundreds of little ones.

It's tempting to say that the point of this book is to demystify BDSM and BDSM relationships, but that's not really it. I like the mystery and I like the surprise in BDSM. I certainly don't want either of these to disappear and then find in their place only clinical analysis and mechanical execution of scenes.

What I'm trying to do here is illuminate the journey but still leave the destinations and waypoints to be just as surprising or mysterious when you get to each one. To use an analogy, if you can clearly see the road then it's easier to choose a good path at each fork than it is in the gloom. When you know the choices you're making are founded on sure knowledge then your anticipation for your next destination builds. If instead you're fumbling in the dark, then disillusionment can easily set in because you don't know if you're making forward progress or whether you're just going in circles.

Understanding the BDSM relationships we have with our partners and with other BDSM folk has to do with understanding the philosophy and psychology of BDSM, and with seeing how what we do fits in with this philosophy and psychology. What we're doing in this second book of this series is taking the theory of book one and seeing how it applies in practice. By couching the practical aspects in good understanding and theory we can dramatically increase the effectiveness of what we do and make it targeted to what we want to achieve.

In a sense, combining the theory and the practical let's us make BDSM less of a hit-and-miss affair[1] and means that we reach

---

[1] Pun intended, of course!

Here's the thing

those surprising and mysterious destinations by design instead of by accident.

Bibliography

[HILL1996]   Hill, Craig A. and Preston, Leslie K. *Individ-ual Differences in the Experience of Sexual Motivation: Theory and Measurements of Dispositional Sexual Motives.* The Journal of Sex Research, volume 33, no. 1, pages 27 – 45, 1996. ISSN 0022-4499

[MASTERS2008] Masters, Peter. *This Curious Human Phenomenon: An exploration of some uncommonly explored aspects of BDSM.* The Nazca Plains Corporation, 2008. ISBN 1-9346-2568-X

[MASTERS2009] Masters, Peter. *The Control Book.* CreateS-pace, 2009. ISBN 1-4421-7386-6

[MESTON2007] Meston, Cindy M. and Buss, David M. *Why Humans Have Sex.* Archives of Sexual Behaviour, volume 36, no. 4, pages 477 – 507, 2007. ISSN 0004-0002

Glossary

24/7   short for 24 hours a day, seven days a week. This refers to a type of D&s or M/s relationship where the two people involved always interact and engage each other in D&s or M/s terms.

BDSM   an acronym for Bondage and Discipline, Dominance and Submission, and Sadism and Masochism.

Bondage   a BDSM activity where a top, dominant, or master uses rope, chain, cuffs or any other method to physically restrain their bottom, submissive, or slave.

Bottom   a BDSM role. A bottom is the one on the receiving end during a BDSM scene such as the one being tied up, the one being struck with a flogger, etc.

Cutting   a BDSM activity using very sharp knives or scalpels to cut designs into the skin. These can be shallow cuts, usually through only a layer or two of skin and which are more for psychological effect than to be actually painful, through to deep cuts which bleed and leave scars.

D&s   a short-hand way to refer to dominant/submissive relationships.

Discipline   any BDSM activity involving an aspect of punishment. Typically things like bare-bottom spanking and caning fall into this category.

Dominant   a BDSM role. A dominant takes charge of some aspect of their partner's activities. This can be solely for the length of a scene, or longer term when they live together.

Dungeon   a special area reserved for BDSM scenes. Usually equipped with specialised and BDSM-adapted furniture such as spanking benches (padded, comfortable benches used during spanking scenes), wooden frames with anchor points used during rope bondage, etc.

Fire play   an activity involving fire, typically where a top applies a thin smear of a volatile liquid—such as an alcohol/water mix—to the skin of a bottom, lights the vapour above the bottom's skin, and then quickly extinguishes the flame to prevent burning.

Flogger   a type of short, multi-tail whip. Usually designed more to thud than sting, the tails are often shorter than one metre and are typically fairly wide and soft. The tails can be made of leather, rope, cord, hair, rubber, etc.

Impact play any BDSM activities where striking one's partner is the goal. Includes slapping, spanking, paddling, whipping, flogging, and so on.

M/s a short-hand way to refer to Master/slave relationships.

Master a BDSM role. A master claims ownership or rights over a slave.

Mistress a BDSM role. Can be the female counterpart of a master, but often this role is merely a female top.

Mummification a type of bondage in which the whole body is encased in a form of wrapping in a manner reminiscent of an egyptian mummy (with holes for breathing, of course). Most commonly the material used for wrapping is something like kitchen cling wrap because it's quick and easy to apply.

Needle play using hypodermic needle tips to thread through the skin, genitals or nipples. Usually done for psychological effect because the needles are actually designed not to hurt (much) unless larger diameters are used. Can also be done for artistic reasons where large numbers of needles are used at one time to create patterns.

Pain play any BDSM activities where causing sharp or dull pain is the goal. Includes caning, whipping, flogging, cutting, etc.

Paddle a paddle similar in shape and size to a ping-pong paddle made out of wood or thick leather. Used for paddling, which is similar to spanking but is done with a paddle instead of a hand.

Play party   a type of BDSM event where people get together to engage in BDSM activities and BDSM play with each other.   Usually held in a private location, such as someone's home, warehouse, loft, or other dedicated space.   Rooms or areas are usually put aside for such play, while other areas are put aside for talking, socialising or eating.

Rope bondage using rope or cord to physically restrain someone partially or fully. Includes full-body bondage, hog-tying, wrist or ankle cuffs made out of rope, etc.

Scene   a collected series of activities with a BDSM focus having a clearly defined start and end;   hence *bondage scene* or *discipline scene*, etc.   Often performed in a dungeon.

               Scene is also sometimes used as a verb meaning to engage in a scene or to perform a scene.   For example, *the dominant intends to scene with his submissive.*

Slave   a BDSM role. A slave assigns ownership or rights over themselves to their partner.

Squick   to cause to feel repulsion, to disgust.

Submissive   a BDSM role. A submissive hands over control over some of their activities to their partner for the length of a scene or longer term if they live together.

Switch   a person who can adopt the role of top or bottom to suit their own and their partner's needs.

Suspension   a type of rope bondage where the person being tied is first tied and is then suspended in the air from a frame or from a bolt in the ceiling.

Top   a BDSM role. A top is the one who does things to their partner, the bottom, during a scene. This could be bondage, spanking, caning, flogging, and so on.

Toys   Equipment used for BDSM play such as floggers, canes, chains, cuffs, etc.; hence *toy bag*, i.e., a bag used for carrying around BDSM equipment.

About the author

Peter Masters is a BDSM dominant and author who lives in Sydney, Australia. He has enjoyed taking control of fine women since his early twenties (which was thirty years ago) and is the author of a number of BDSM and kinky-sex-related books.

He has a website, which is more a wiki than anything else, where you can find hundreds of articles on BDSM and related topics:

`http://www.peter-masters.com/`